THE AIRSTREAM THAT RAN AWAY WITH THE SPOON

The Airstream That Ran Away with the Spoon

Printed in the United States of America
ISBN 978-1-946425-37-9

Book Design by CSinclaire Write-Design
Book Cover Art by James Hislope

• WRITE WAY •
PUBLISHING COMPANY
RALEIGH, NORTH CAROLINA

THANK YOU TO . . .

John, who has supported me in all of my activities for almost a decade, even when I decided to move into an RV three days after learning that was a thing.

My father and my late mother, who provided the opportunities that I've had, and Betsy who with my father is building their own new story.

Marcia, who keeps my business from falling into chaos.

Happy the rabbit, who accompanied me on this journey.

The many people who contributed to the publication of this book including Lee, Villate, Jessica, and too many others to name.

THE AIRSTREAM THAT RAN AWAY WITH THE SPOON

DISCOVERING A NEW HOME AND A NEW LIFE WITH CHRONIC FATIGUE

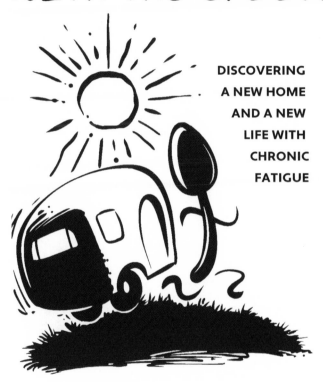

MARY K.D. D'ROZARIO

• WRITE WAY •
PUBLISHING COMPANY
RALEIGH, NORTH CAROLINA

Contents

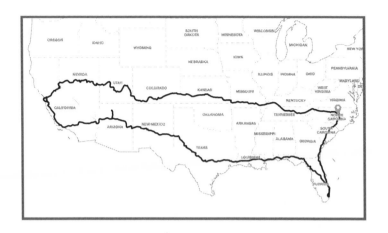

CHAPTER 1

Admit You're Sick

A COUPLE OF YEARS BEFORE THIS STORY starts, I was at a networking event in Research Triangle Park, North Carolina, when the room began to go black and I found I couldn't stand up. I collapsed onto a nearby bench and asked someone to bring me water. For the rest of the evening, I stayed in that one spot, smiling and chatting with friends who came by. I had been in the biotechnology field for almost twenty years, had been an entrepreneur for a few recent years, was an occasional sponsor of the event being held that night, and was on the board of the organization that hosted it.

What my peers didn't know was that I had become an entrepreneur because I could no longer be as successful at my job as I wanted to be. Though I got top reviews, no one knew I couldn't stay awake for eight hours at a time. As a home-based employee, I was sleeping several hours in the middle of the day. I slept next to my phone and computer so I could snap to attention if anyone called. No one seemed to notice, but I knew I couldn't keep up the charade.

When I became an entrepreneur with several clients, I continued to keep up appearances. If I didn't answer their calls or emails right away, my clients just assumed I was working on another client's tasks. And if I was sleeping in the middle of the day, so what, that was my own business so long as I got my work done. As I spent more and more time at various medical appointments, "meetings" with some other client filled my calendar. One of my clients congratulated me that my business must be very successful with so many client meetings.

In the winter, I slept most of the day. My employees who were picking up the slack started asking if this was the year I was finally going to move to Florida for the winter. The problem was, I wasn't making enough money to keep my house near my clients and friends, my business and social network, and my boyfriend, John, in Research Triangle Park and also have an apartment in South Florida, where I needed to spend the winter to alleviate my symptoms. To be honest, between my work hour limitations and the $24,000 insurance and medical expenses that final year at home, I wasn't making enough money to keep my house at all.

Meanwhile, my employees and I tried to keep my customers and business network from knowing just how sick I was. Because my business network made up a large portion of my social network, I couldn't share what I was going through with my friends. Business is a snake pit, I had been told. If you should never let them see you sweat, you certainly should never let them see you pass out. And never, never let them see that you don't have enough money to live in your own house.

It was only when I started to write this book, more than a year after moving out of my house, that John realized I had sold my house because I had to. Like so many other people who manage to keep working while dealing with chronic illness, I felt that keeping my struggles a secret was my only hope for future success.

With this book, I'm going to break the rules. Over this year of living in an RV, I learned to break a lot of business and RVing rules in order to thrive in my new life. Indeed, thriving in an RV meant learning to break the rules about illness itself. Every story in this book shares lessons, some crucial and some trivial, that I have learned about how to live in an RV and how living in an RV can be made to work for someone with an illness that causes chronic fatigue.

For several reasons, I won't be discussing my specific diseases and medical conditions. Instead, I will just call the whole mess "my illness." One reason is that now or in the future I may be paid to promote awareness of certain diseases by biotechnology companies. This is how I make my living. I have to follow the complex regulations governing the biotechnology industry to disclose these relationships when I talk about specific diseases and treatments.

Another reason is my own privacy. I live in a nation that can't figure out whether I'm going to be able to purchase health insurance and access care or not. I have also found that I live in a society full of people who were short-changed when they were handed manners. The saying "my health is not your small talk" needs to be hung up in a few more classrooms and embroidered on many more tea towels.

I want to emphasize that my story is not unique. Though no one knows exactly how many people live full-time in RVs ("recreational vehicles" that may be vans, motor homes, or travel trailers) in the United States, more than two million RVs are on the road and pretty much every parking lot and campground has someone who is full-time.

Safe to say, there are a lot of us. There is nothing more obnoxious than a full-time RVer who thinks they are fascinating to other full-time RVers, and I don't want to be that person. Many people, some with YouTube channels and many quietly living private lives, share my experiences.

Adding to the potential obnoxiousness of my

story, there is also little more obnoxious than a sick person who is held up as an example of what other sick people can or should do. Please don't use my story to do that. Everyone with chronic fatigue seeks alternatives that allow richness in a limited life, and it is safe to say that every single one of us has encountered people who think we aren't doing enough. What they will never know is that we ask ourselves if we are doing enough every day. Until we understood we were sick, we may have beaten ourselves up, not understanding how we could possibly be so much lazier than everyone else.

One time, before I realized how sick I was, I was at a client meeting that had run all day. It was now evening, and we were supposed to be calling taxis and returning to our hotel, but everyone kept talking. I felt like I was being tortured, and I eventually blew up in a most unprofessional manner. The taxis were called immediately! I got to go to bed while the rest of the team went out to dinner.

Once when an actual direct symptom of my illness appeared in a meeting, I was later called in by my manager and told that I—really my disease—had been rude. I wasn't in a place to recognize that I was sick, much less communicate that to anyone else.

In the past, when I failed to do the things other people could do, the only reason I could come up with was that I just didn't have as much grit as everyone else, despite the fact that throughout my life it is clear that I have quite a bit of grit. It was a confusing time.

I am fortunate in that I have specific issues that show up on lab results and other medical tests that explain my illness. I've encountered bizarre reactions to my symptoms from doctors, along with stunningly incorrect diagnoses and terrible advice, but never disbelief. But the most important person to receive those laboratory results and to see on paper that I really am sick is me. Too many people with chronic fatigue don't have this gift granted to them.

I've learned that there's nothing wrong with my character and, if there is something wrong with my personality, profound laziness or a lack of grit isn't it. I feel for sick people who don't have the advantage of laboratory results that show they are sick, not just for the questions and judgment they get from physicians and other people but for the kind of questioning that goes on in their own hearts.

Many people with illnesses that are different or worse than mine are physically or financially limited from dragging their bed around everywhere they go, as I do with my RV. They may be limited in acting on their own dreams, whatever the dreams may be. They may require round-the-clock care and be unable to perform any of the activities of daily life at all. This isn't from a lack of desire or a lack of willpower; it is because they are sick. Even without my illness, the universal experience of aging will end my own ability to live in my current RV choice at some point. But for now, this is what is working for me.

Sometimes people with chronic fatigue feel pressure to pretend to have a limp to show how sick they really are. It can be uncomfortable to rise out of a wheelchair in front of people who don't understand that it isn't that you can't walk, it's just that you can't walk that far. Or that you can't walk and also have enough energy to negotiate difficult work conversations. I have no idea what it would be like to have a leg that didn't work but still have all of your energy. That person's experience of disability is very different from mine.

People with chronic fatigue often identify as "spoonies" after an essay titled "The Spoon Theory" by Christine Miserandino. In this essay, available on the Internet for free, the author explains that portioning out your energy is like using up spoons. Once you are out of spoons, that's all you can do for the day. Some feel that the theory doesn't explain chronic fatigue very well, preferring other metaphors such as a gas tank.

For me, the essay is both gut wrenching and a perfect description of my experience. One thing she describes is how jealously we have to guard our extra spoons in case something goes wrong. Sometimes all of my spoons disappear into thin air, and I'm left with nothing but a sensation that I'm about to hit the deck, or vomit, or both.

Hopefully when that happens I'm close to my bed and my bed is close to a legal parking place. If it's not, I have to conjure up one more spoon or I could get hurt. Or arrested. Law enforcement encounters are a continual risk to people with disabilities. In this book, I will describe my own brush with terrifying and demeaning harassment.

CHAPTER 2

Finding My RV

TRAVEL IS NOT NEW TO ME. MY FAVORITE job I ever had involved flying all around North America. I won an award from my company for going to the most places in one year. I found out I had gone twice as many places as the next person. It wasn't unusual for a week to include an itinerary with stops as geographically diverse as Winnipeg, Los Angeles, and Miami.

Back then, I was the most energized I had ever been in my life. I lost almost 100 pounds and participated in half marathons and sprint triathlons that I worked into my travel schedule. But this was also when the problems with my health started to accelerate. I was passing out regularly. Sometimes I couldn't think coherently for hours or even days after exercise.

One day while I was sitting at my desk, my heart rate reached 130 beats per minute. I drove straight to my doctor's office, where I got a lecture about calling 911 and was given some medication to take for the rest of my life. Later, my heart developed an odd rhythm. This time I drove to the emergency room down the street from my house. I got the same lecture about calling 911 and more lifetime medication but no solutions to my accelerating health crisis.

Meanwhile, each winter I went into a kind of hibernation. As my health situation deteriorated, I started to think seriously about wintering in Florida. For two years I thought about it, but I couldn't find a solution.

When I had traveled to Florida for work, I had driven past fields and fields of RVs. I thought wintering in an RV might be the answer, but I quickly learned that winter lot rents in Florida were as much as my mortgage. Part-time living in an RV wouldn't solve the problem of maintaining my home in North Carolina and also being able to afford to winter in Florida. But as I was looking into the option, I learned about people who work from home while living in their RVs. I started watching their YouTube videos. Three days after learning that people live in RVs, I decided I was going to be one of them.

I'm a quick decision maker. In "Bad Choices and Bad Advice" I'll talk about "maximizers" and whether that strategy, which I don't use, works well for someone with chronic fatigue. Decision-making is sometimes described as a process that involves contemplating, preparing, experimenting, and doing. I have always skipped the experimenting phase and gone straight to doing. This approach allowed me to fit several amazing lives into this lifetime before I got sick, creating experiences I will always be grateful to have had. And now that I am simply unable to expend the energy required for experimenting, my process still serves me well.

It is no small matter to say that RV videos on YouTube changed my life and perhaps even saved my life. I learned about a way of living that would work for me, and I was able to shop for an RV without ever leaving my couch because any possible RV has multiple walkthrough videos and reviews on YouTube. This was essential because attending a large RV show would be impossible for me.

People who live in RVs make videos about their days and weeks and years living full-time in an RV. Throughout this book, I will reference my favorite YouTube channels, and I encourage you to check them out even if you're not planning to live in an RV—these are great people.

Every last person I know told me to try renting an RV first to see if I like it. People say that all the time. People with experience with RVs don't want you to make a mistake. People without experience with RVs are afraid of trailer parks. This is one of the rules I broke.

I don't have the energy for experiments. Chronic fatigue means I live life in the final draft.

Besides, what was the point of renting an RV? Renting an RV meant trying a model that I wasn't going to buy, staying in an RV park convenient to my then-home that I wouldn't otherwise stay in, and spending a week of exhausted discombobulation from having moved into a place that I would be moving out of. And it would probably take me several weeks to recover from all of that.

I'm not sure if I was a snob or if I just like nice RVs, but I was drawn to the Airstream that I saw in the YouTube channels of Less Junk, More Journey and A Streamin' Life. I was also enamored of the T@B seen in the YouTube videos of Mandy Lea Photo and an episode of the Bob Wells YouTube channel, CheapRVliving. The model T@B I wanted had a tiny kitchen across the front, a tiny wet bath (where you shower over the toilet), and a dinette that was also a bed. One person could make the back of the dinette into a twin-size bed and still leave chairs at a desk-sized table.

I knew I wanted a travel trailer. If your tow vehicle (the vehicle used to tow the trailer) breaks, you can park your trailer at an RV park and wait for your vehicle to be repaired. The vehicle can be repaired at most any repair shop instead of the kind of specialty shops required to repair a motor home. Also, I was sick. I wanted small and simple. I didn't want slides or complications. And I wanted something nice—something that I would feel proud to live in.

Most RVs don't feel nice. Keeping the two models I liked in mind, on July 4th weekend, John took me to the two local dealers that carried each brand of trailer. While at the dealers, we looked at other trailers and found walls that were made of cardboard. We joked about how my pet rabbit, Happy, could eat right through them. In fact, people who store their RVs sometimes find them remodeled by rats.

When it came to Airstream, the Flying Cloud 25-foot model seemed perfect to live in, but it was more than I could afford. Maybe with more time and the energy to fly across the country to look at one, I could have found a used one. Anyway, at 25 feet it was longer than what I had in mind. Part of the reason I liked the T@B was that it was shorter than a car, which meant I could park by pulling through a double parking space. I pictured myself working at Starbucks with my house in the parking lot outside. The 25-foot model was just too big.

I wasn't sure about Airstream's Sport 16-foot model, but it was what I could afford. Unlike the T@B, I could stand up in it. It had a place to work, a bed, a kitchen, and a wet bath. A space under the bed for storage would be a perfect hidey-hole for Happy. I measured, and one side of the dinette could be pulled out and replaced with a Herman Miller office chair. With so many problems with my body, that chair seemed like one of the most important things from the house to take with me.

John convinced me to look at the next model up,

the Airstream Sport 22. Its narrow center aisle left me uncomfortable. As a plus-size woman, I found the Sport 16 with its open center space to be much more comfortable. I decided I would buy the Sport 16.

The problem was, RVing was taking off in popularity and the Sport 16 was a very popular model. There wasn't one in the entire country that wasn't already spoken for. The waiting list at the factory was months. When an Airstream Sport 16 finally became available to purchase, it had a solar panel on the roof. I was very frustrated. I didn't have a lot of cargo weight to work with as it was, and I didn't want the weight of the solar panel to reduce the little I had.

After asking for an hour to think about the solar panel, however, I made the down payment on the Airstream Sport 16. That doesn't mean I didn't keep looking at other RVs every night. I still do. And the solar panel turned out to be a fantastic piece of luck. I'll be talking more about my adventures with solar later in this book.

Owning an Airstream is owning a piece of Americana. I had not known what an Airstream was before I started looking for an RV. I do not remember ever seeing one. But now Airstream lore is a part of me, and I love living in such a beautiful piece of American history. My previous home had been decorated to reflect a specific period of American history, and I get to have that all over again with the Airstream.

People love an Airstream, even if they don't know what it is. Anywhere I stop, from gas stations to grocery stores, the Airstream gets comments. People tend to assume it is an antique and are often surprised that Airstreams are still made.

I also needed a vehicle to tow the Airstream. Because I wanted my things to be inside, I decided to get an SUV. The Expedition had the highest tow capacity in its class, and though my advisors didn't recommend it, it could tow the 25-foot Airstream if I just couldn't stand the Sport 16 and decided to go up in size. It could easily tow the Airstream Sport 16.

I decided to get a model that was a few years old, had the tow package, four-wheel drive, and the extra-long storage area in the back. At any given time, there were only one or two cars meeting my requirements available anywhere in the country. I ordered one that was particularly desirable because of its low mileage. It was accidentally shipped to the wrong dealership and then sold to someone else. A few weeks later two more became available, and the dealership had both shipped to North Carolina for me to inspect.

The year before I had to sell a truck that I had purchased new almost 20 years ago. My mechanic advised me that my many years of trouble-free ownership were coming to an end and that I should trade it in before it completely broke down. With all the other loss I was experiencing, I had been heartbroken at losing a vehicle I had owned for so long. One of the Expeditions smelled exactly like my old truck, as if the spirit of my truck had come back to take care of me. That's the one I selected.

Combined, the Expedition and the Sport 16 make up my "rig." As an RVer, my rig is who I am. This is what people see about me everywhere I go.

In the year that followed, I ended up spending a lot of time on federal land and got good use out of the four-wheel drive. The extra-long storage has been perfect for carrying my belongings. The low gas mileage is a negative, but I'm not sure a smaller car would have worked for me even though I stayed with the smaller trailer. I'm always at the weight limit of the Expedition.

At first, I thought I was making a compromise by selecting the Airstream Sport 16. In exchange for a lower price and being able to do U-turns, I had very little space and a wet bath. Within the first week, I didn't see it as a compromise anymore. The Airstream Sport 16 is the right size for me, and I love the self-cleaning bathroom.

In the Sport 16, there's no hallway aside from the central space that is used for everything, no space behind the toilet that isn't used, nothing extra. Everything in the trailer is used all the time. You clean it as you use it, so there's nothing extra to do. I found that it is perfect for living with my illness.

The wet bath means that you have a large space to take your shower and, I learned, you take your shower sitting down. Later on, I read a book about my illness that recommended sitting showers so you don't waste what little energy you have on your shower. Perfect!

The only thing that gets to me every once in a while is that the kitchen is very small. I have no oven, which I make up for with an Instant Pot—more on that later. As nice as a larger kitchen would be, though, it wouldn't make up for losing all the convenience I have in my tiny trailer.

I did have some other options. The legal definition of an RV (and tiny houses end up in the same category) is basically housing that is less than 400 square feet. Within these parameters, RVs come in several classes with motors in addition to the bumper-pull trailers and fifth wheels that require a tow vehicle.

Class A RVs are the big boxes you see going down the freeway. Some are small, but generally they are larger and heavier. They're more like a house inside, with all the house things to clean. But they often have automatic jacks (right now I have to hand crank my levelers) and other features that make them easier to set up.

Class B RV's are vans. I love the idea of a van, but at my size I don't think I would ever find a van I was comfortable in. I've tried them out, and in some of them I can't even close the door on the shower. There's also a new category, B+, which are vans whose walls have been customized to go straight up instead of curving in giving a little bit more room.

Class C RV's keep the cab area of the vehicle they were customized from, and then the back is all house, frequently with an area that extends over the cab. In addition to those categories, there are also some other options like truck campers and specialty trailer designs that are part tent.

With some other RVs, people tow a car behind

known as a "towed" (or "toad"). With a travel trailer, I feel like you have a towed that is no inconvenience at all and then magically you have a car. A travel trailer means owning and maintaining just one engine. And while my current total length hitched up is 35 feet, an equivalent 35 feet of RV isn't as maneuverable.

Unless a towed is completely on a trailer, it can't back up. The "tail swing" on a large RV means it can't get through tight areas like urban parking lots. I don't have any of those problems. With my hitch pivot in the middle of my 35 feet, I can wriggle through like a centipede. The ability to drive anywhere without worrying about getting trapped in a tight parking lot or dead-end street has a lot going for it.

It's difficult to imagine any other kind of RV when my current trailer is perfect, but at some point, I may have trouble hitching or cranking down the stabilizers and may have to think about something else. When that happens, I will give up some of my current conveniences.

Full-time RVers, no matter what their health status, tend to move from RV to RV. It isn't necessarily because the first RV was the wrong RV but rather because wants and needs change.

No one can give you good advice about which RV you as an individual should live in. All I can say about advice is that if you want to know what it is like to live in a particular RV, ask people who live in it. When someone asks about my RV or RVs like it on social media, the comments are overwhelmingly from people who have never lived in one saying how terrible it would be.

Even if you don't ask, you still might get advice. It is not uncommon to walk outside in an RV park and find a full-time RVer who thinks he's fascinating holding court with the mere weekenders, explaining why a full-timer must have a class A. If my RV isn't right for him, what does he know about it? More about bad advice later.

CHAPTER 3

Disability Means
Losing Everything

MY EXPERIENCE OF DISABILITY HAS BEEN fundamentally about loss. This book is about how I lost my house and most of my possessions. Sometimes people say to me that I'm "lucky" to live in an RV. Luck has nothing to do with it. I am able to live in an RV because I was able to endure what I had to give up.

In middle class America, people are not used to having to make these choices. The discomfort of giving up a thing that you sort of like because you have to make a choice isn't something that happens in most people's lives. Walk into many homes and you will see that people have become so uncomfortable giving things up that they are keeping literal trash.

Some people can't learn to navigate the discomfort of giving up things that they love. I know people who had every intention of moving into an RV, but when it came to getting rid of their belongings, they couldn't do it. When you speak to people who live in RVs, almost everyone has a story to tell about how they got through this point in the process.

My secret weapon until I got sick had always been my tenacity. I had to take early childhood trauma and a disastrous marriage at a young age and become a success armed with nothing but a philosophy degree. I did it, growing a career in the biotechnology industry, because I could work harder than everyone else.

My tenacity became dulled by my ever-present exhaustion, but I still wanted to win at life. I had always said that "Mary always wins," but I wasn't saying it now. How could I win any more?

I thought I had become inflexible. I used to fly everywhere for work, and now I was so cautious about doing anything. I thought maybe that's just what happens as you get older. Isn't that the normal thing? You get set in your ways and don't want to try new things. I didn't understand that it was my illness that made me cautious. I didn't understand that flexibility had become my new secret weapon.

I found that I had the ability to be so flexible that

I could curl completely around my loss and come out in front of it. That's what I did when I sold everything to move into this RV. The fact that I could find the emotional strength to walk away from everything I owned was the only way I could win, and I doubled down on it in the largest way possible.

You can find quite a few essays and YouTube videos from full-time RVers about how they learned to let go of their things and win. Marie Kondo's book, *The Magical Art of Tidying Up*, is somewhat helpful, but her book is mainly about learning to get rid of trash. Learning to let go of things that you love and that are useful is a different kind of letting go.

Over the several years that I was working up to being able to let go of my things, I had come to feel completely trapped by my house. I lived in a three-story townhouse with the bedrooms on the top and the washer and dryer on the bottom. It had three toilets and two showers to keep clean. Even if I wanted to continue to be a homeowner, it was a disastrously wrong house for me.

Nevertheless, I was unable to take any action. I didn't have the energy to move to another house. I probably couldn't get a mortgage. Bizarrely, I had never in my life rented an apartment and that seemed daunting and intrusive and impossible. What is everyone who is sick afraid of? Becoming homeless. Well, death first. But after that, homelessness.

Consequently, in my mind, hanging onto that house was the most important thing in making sure I had housing and food and health insurance. It contained the spirit of my safety, and I couldn't let go. It felt profoundly irresponsible to let go.

At one point my house had been the right house for me. I had loved this house. I had a thing about the 1880s and had customized my townhouse until it was unrecognizable as a modern build. I had divided the kitchen from the living room with a wall of stained glass, installed crown molding, put up busy wallpaper, and crammed every inch of it with antiques.

Then, in a moment, it became apparent to me that I could sell it. On the previous day it had been impossible, and the next day it was the obvious solution. It was one of those mental transformations that you can never force a person to have, that you can't even force yourself to have. Some kind of grace enters your mind, and what was impossible becomes possible.

At that point I just wanted it gone. Everyone asked why I was in such a rush. I had not yet met anyone who had started the process of moving into an RV and not made it, but I could imagine it happening. I had a swell of intention in me that had come to me through grace. If it left, I had no process for getting it back. And what would I do if my intention—or my luck—gave out and I was caught in some kind of impossible in-between place? Right now, today, was my chance.

There was so much that could go wrong. The economy was high, and houses were selling quickly, but that could change. My health could change. My own economic situation could worsen. Indeed, shortly after I moved into my RV, some conflicts developed with a major client, and we eventually decided to part ways. If that had happened before I moved, I'm not sure what I would have done.

The rush also gave me a distraction from the discomfort of whittling through my things. If someone wanted something I had, for the most part I just let it go. I took piles of stuff down the street to Goodwill and shipped boxes off to friends. I shipped forty pounds of boxes of unsorted stuff to a friend, assuming she would find something in there she wanted and get rid of the rest.

For an entire group of other items, I simply avoided making decisions for a year. Things I didn't want any more but that had value were crammed into boxes marked "E" for "eBay." I got the largest storage locker available.

Yes, I paid storage for a year on things I never intended to keep. There are plenty of people who would advise against that, and it would be good advice. You know what else is good advice? Keep moving while you have the momentum to finish a project.

By keeping the storage locker, I thought I was giving myself an out. If things didn't work with the RV, I would still have my furniture and a lot of my things. I probably had at least $20,000 in furniture and home furnishings. When it came time to get rid of it, the value on the used market was less than $1,000. All of America is downsizing, and no one wants your old furniture.

At the time, I was healthy enough that over several weeks I managed to package everything I owned into boxes by myself. I hired a very energetic moving team who filled the storage locker with hardly an inch to spare.

By the time moving was completed, I could feel one leg and one foot, not on the same side of my body, but I had succeeded. It turned out to have been a good choice. The economy held, but my health did not.

I was out of my house, but my RV wasn't ready yet. I had found an apartment sublet from people who were buying their own home, but their purchase fell through, and I lost the opportunity. The fee for a long-term stay hotel was double with a pet and therefore unaffordable. I ended up staying in John's house for three months.

We had been together seven years and never lived together because we don't want to live together. I had an enormous power of intention behind me to get my house sold and get into this RV. He had a freeloader blocking his driveway and getting annoyed when the TV was on late. We're still unpacking that experience.

I had lived in my house for over 10 years, and it was in no condition to be sold. I had thought that I would be able to get my money out of it with an "as is" sale, especially with the economy so hot that homes in my neighborhood were selling in a day. However, a neighbor tried to sell an "as is" house and it didn't sell.

Part of the reason I wanted to be able to sell and walk away was because I was certain I was going to be heartbroken as the stained glass and wallpaper came down and the white box of the original style reemerged. In reality, as soon as those embellishments were gone, it was no longer "my house." I had no emotional attachment to it at that point and going through the process of removing every trace of my personality from the home was easy.

Well, it was easy for me. The guy who had to take down all the wallpaper had some regrets! I also had to have all of the flooring replaced and upgrade the counters from the laminate that had been just fine for me. I was able to leave all of the appliances for the new owner and also one large item of furniture that worked particularly well with the house.

The house sold in three days, which distressed me enormously at the time. Why was my house taking so long to sell?! The buyer produced a laundry list of improvements needed for the house. We made a price concession to make all of that go away, and I was finally free of the house.

I wasn't quite free of my belongings, but they were out of sight thanks to the almost $200 a month storage locker bill. Plenty of people can criticize that bill, but it meant I could move on with my life. As the commercial says, some things are priceless.

A year later, I came back to downsize to a smaller storage locker. That week I was having trouble with my arms. I thought the problem was going to be permanent. It turned out to be temporary, but if it had happened when I was trying to move out of my house, it would have made my plans a disaster. Fortunately, I had hired a very patient man who was used to working with the elderly on estate sales as they navigated their own loss, and he was perfect for me.

He brought each box to me to decide to eBay it or keep it and took a piece of furniture in exchange for moving everything I kept into a smaller storage locker. I got 50 percent of the money from what was sold on eBay. The process was pretty easy; I had made my decisions a year ago when I marked the boxes "E" or something else. After not seeing things for a year and having enjoyed what giving those things up could mean to me, I was ready to add even more to the "E" pile.

These are the things I kept: most of my library, a couple of pieces of furniture, family heirlooms, some art that wasn't worth enough to sell but was meaningful in some way, framed pictures, and some things I had collected in my world travels. About half of the volume of my belongings is my library.

Where I am now is that I am paying about $1,000 a year to keep my library and these other things. I'm sure someone else could do better, but it's the best I can do. My library is not something I'm ready to lose. Getting rid of everything else meant I could make that choice.

CHAPTER 4

RV Living Day Zero

WHILE I WAS WAITING THINGS OUT AT JOHN'S house, my Airstream Sport 16 was having a hard time. It had an accident on the way to the dealer and had to go back to the factory for repairs. After three months, I finally got the call that it had arrived at the dealer and would be ready to pick up in a week.

RVs are not produced with the same attention to detail as cars. Manufacturing quality techniques such as Six Sigma that are standard in other industries haven't made their way into the RV industry. To make up for that manufacturing shortcoming, a good dealer will go over every system and make sure the RV is in working order before they hand it over to their customer. While new RVs are known for having a lot of problems, either I lucked out or my dealer was especially thorough in their inspection. My Airstream, which I had already named the Halfloaf, has had almost no problems.

For the week between getting the call and moving in, all I had was my VIN. I called my insurance agent and arranged coverage. Most RV policies limit the number of days per year that the RV can be used, so I had to get a special policy for full-time living. Because of the weird economics of RVs at the time, immediately available used units were sometimes selling for even more than new units, so I chose to have replacement coverage.

I was so excited when I received my insurance card that I put a picture on the special (secret) Facebook photo album I had started. The photo album was secret because I had encountered some disturbing reactions from people who knew my plans. I have, over the course of my life, encountered some very good fortune. At one point, I had a fairly high salary and was able to go to many places in the world. I purchased art and a luxury car. Despite all of those experiences, nothing I have done has engendered the naked jealously I faced when I told people I was moving into an RV.

A lot of people are where I was before that moment of grace. They are trapped in their lives and see no possible way out. While some people truly are trapped, such as those whose disabilities have left them with no financial resources, the people I was talking to were colleagues from the biotechnology industry. They had the education and financial means to make any possible choice available to them. And yet, as mysterious and unresolved as my situation had been for me just a few months earlier, they too looked around and saw no choices for themselves. My choice, once I made it, became a focus of their helpless rage.

I quickly learned that it was better to just keep things to myself. Why did you sell the house? Oh, I decided to spend some time in Florida. Where do you live now? With my boyfriend. Are you going to buy another house? I'm not sure yet, I'm figuring things out.

But things were figured out! The last few days were like waiting for Christmas morning. Finally, it was the morning to pick up my trailer. Everything had to go just right because I had to be at a conference in South Florida three days later. I got up early and packed my last few things in my car. Happy was going to stay with John until after the conference.

When I arrived at the Airstream dealer, someone took my car to set up my hitch while I signed all the paperwork. Most bumper-pulled RV hitches use a weight distribution system that transfers some of the RV weight to the front tires of the vehicle. This makes it safer to drive. Because my car is bigger than my trailer, in my case weight also transfers back to the trailer so my weight distribution system has to remain fairly loose. I use it because of the increased stability it offers.

Some weight distribution systems have an anti-sway feature built in, but mine does not. Therefore, I have a second device, called an anti-sway bar, that I also use. The anti-sway bar helps prevent a dangerous situation where the trailer can get into an increasing sway pattern—for example, after being hit by a strong gust of wind—that can eventually pull the back end of the car over and lead to a serious wreck.

The Airstream dealer had a tech show me how everything worked. He was an old-timer who knew absolutely everything there was to know about Airstreams. He was also active on one of the RV social media groups I had found to be the most unpleasant. While he just liked to answer questions and help people, the forum included a lot of drama that I did not enjoy.

Baby boomers, not being digital natives, don't have a lot of art to how they behave online. They don't troll or shitpost. When they are rude and mean online, they tend to be rude and mean in exactly the same way a person might experience in real life. Somehow this strikes me as worse. Yet, as a person who lives in an RV, their corner of the Internet is often where I need to go to get the answers I need.

The tech was adamant that his demo would be better than anything I had seen on YouTube. That wasn't really possible in just an hour or two, but he did check off every system he was supposed to show me. He even walked me through setting out my awning twice, but this process continued to completely baffle me. Whenever I wanted to put out my awning, I would have to bring up a YouTube video and pause it after each step. It was only after living in the Airstream for almost an entire year that I was reliably able to put out my awning without the help of anyone from YouTube.

I drove once around a small block with the tech in my car, I guess to make sure I wasn't manifestly unsafe pulling a trailer, and that was it. My insurance carrier had also wanted to know if I had ever pulled a trailer before. I had—more than 20 years ago when I was a teenager on the family cattle ranch. That was enough to get insurance. For someone who might want to actually know what they're doing before they drive their RV, there are classes available. I eventually figured things out without harming any people or Airsteams. Flying to a class would have taken more energy than I had available.

As I left the dealership, I knew I was not ready to get on the freeway. The freeway onramp was only a few hundred yards from the dealer. I turned the opposite direction down the road with no plan except to stay between the lines. Fortunately, there were no dead ends or I would have been stuck; it wasn't until a few months later that I learned to back up. On the way down to Florida, I took a wrong exit off the freeway and had to drive 20 miles out of my way to get back onto the freeway because I couldn't turn around.

CHAPTER 5

How to Make Water Go Uphill

I HEADED TO A NEARBY KOA TO SPEND THE night. KOAs are a chain of campgrounds, frequently located near freeways exits. They are set up well to deal with people who don't know how to work their RVs. They usually have a lot of pull-through sites so you don't have to know how to back up and a lot of workampers ready to help you. (Workampers are people who live in RVs and go to jobs, such as working at KOAs, that are specifically designed for people who live in RVs.)

People in RV parks tend to be helpful to the nth degree. Really all you need to do is stand around looking lost and someone will offer to help. Sometimes they want to help when you don't even want help, like after you learn how to back up on your own. For now, though, I wanted all the help.

I had to unhitch in order to open the huge tailgate on my Expedition and unload my bedding and everything that belonged in the trailer, but I couldn't get my hitch undone. It took everything one of the workampers had, but he was able to get it disconnected. It was the only time I would unhitch for a while—more on that later.

The night after I picked up my trailer was the first night I ever stayed in an RV as an adult. My Airstream trailer requires three physical tasks from me: hitching and dealing with the stabilizers (feet that crank down under the trailer), driving, and connecting the water and the sewer. After watching hours of YouTube videos, I had a handle on all three of these tasks and was able to complete them successfully on the first try. Over time, I would learn to do all three more efficiently and work out a plan of attack so they would have the least impact on my chronic fatigue. Soon, however, I would learn I was missing a basic skill: how to make water go uphill.

The next morning, I decided to dump my sewer tank. I have no idea why I decided to do that. Now I usually hitch and dump on different days because each takes a toll on my energy, but I didn't have a "usually" yet. I had only been there one day. I only need to dump every few days, but maybe I didn't know that. For whatever reason, I really wanted to dump my sewer tank.

Most RVs have a fresh water tank and then two other tanks, one for the toilet and one for the shower and sinks. This is something of a holdover from a time when RVs were used differently. Some people who have RVs with this configuration add connections to combine their tanks. My tiny RV has only one combined tank. When I tried to dump it, I encountered a problem I didn't know how to deal with: the sewer connection was uphill from my trailer. I had no idea how to make water flow uphill.

I went down to the office and asked if I could dump after I circled around on the road. They said no, that it was just fine to dump where I was. Yes, but how? In general, people were very helpful, and on this first stay, these people had already been very helpful with the hitch and everything.

But they seemed to find making water flow uphill such an obvious skill that they couldn't even begin to explain it to me. "When you're finished just pick up the end of the tube and all the water will go in the sewer," they said. I was still puzzled, but they seemed confident that it would all work out and clearly the conversation was over.

I went back to my trailer and surveyed the situation. When I unhooked the end of the tube from the trailer, how was I going to pick it up fast enough that the sewage wouldn't just come pouring out? It made no sense to me, but they had said it would work.

It didn't work. As soon as I twisted off the sewer tube, sewage came pouring out. I quickly reattached it. I thought some more. I didn't see any other solution, and they had said it would work. I twisted off the sewer tube and more sewage came out. After a couple of rounds of this, all the sewage was on the ground. Which, if nothing else, solved the problem of emptying my tank.

Now I just wanted to get out of there as fast as possible before anyone saw or smelled what I had done. I was headed to Florida, and I wasn't going to have to see any of these people again for a long time. I started the car and headed for the freeway.

By the time I came back, I had learned to make water go uphill. The solution is called "slinkying." You need to park close enough to the sewer drain that you have some give in your sewer tube. Then you can lift the tube from the RV end and slinky the water through to the drain end. After a few times, the tube will be mostly empty and nothing will spill when you twist it off of the RV. Today I am such an expert at making water flow uphill that I never give it a second thought. But if a newbie asked me how on earth to make water go uphill, I would certainly understand what they meant!

That first dump was the only time I could get my sewer hose connected to the RV. The standard sewer hose set up for RVs requires twisting L-shaped "bay-onets" over posts. My illness has left me with limited use of my hands and this isn't something I can do easily. As proof that RVers will help you with truly anything, someone offered to connect my sewer line for me every time for my next few stops.

Eventually, I purchased a file, and now each time I buy a new sewer tube, the first thing I do is file down the bayonets until I can easily attach the sewer line myself. I have also found that leaving the sewer tube in the sun to soften makes it easier to connect. A hair dryer works too. People get antsy if they see a sewer line stretched out on the ground, so if I can't get mine on, I just leave it partially twisted on and come back later to get it the rest of the way.

The only other time over the following year I wasn't able to get my sewer tube connected was when my leg was not working properly and I wasn't able to get into the right position to put my body weight into twisting the connection. Airstreams are unusually low to the ground, which makes them great for someone who has trouble with stairs. But it also means I usually have to get on my knees to connect the sewer tube. If the ground is clean, I put my front door mat under my knees. If it isn't clean, like a dump station, I use a plastic trash bag laid out on the ground.

The design of the standard RV sewer connection is difficult for many kinds of disabilities. As the RV industry becomes more responsive to the needs of people with disabilities, hopefully they will come up with a better type of connection.

By the way, realizing that I have only lived in an RV for a year, you might wonder why I have to keep buying sewer tubes. The reason is that landscapers with weedwhackers like to turn sewer tubes into sprinklers.

The holes from the tips of the weedwhacker strings are so tiny that you don't see them until you lean over your sewer tube and open the valve. Just part of the fun of RVing.

CHAPTER 6

A Bad Hombre and a Bad Omen

I HAD STUFFED IN SOME DENTAL WORK before I left town. As a result, a symptom of my illness that I hadn't experienced in years developed as I was driving south. As I drove, I ran my tongue over the hard lumps in my mouth caused by my illness. The lumps were small and didn't really matter, but every time my tongue ran over them, it was reminder that I couldn't drive away from whatever future my body has in store for me.

I was also driving toward the destruction left behind by Hurricane Irma. As I was heading south to the conference in Boca Raton, the power was out and the conference hotel wouldn't give a final green light for the conference. It struck me as perhaps very stupid that I was taking my new home into Florida during hurricane season.

I didn't stay in the Halfloaf during the conference. When I had made my travel plans, I had never lived in an RV, and I wasn't sure how easy it would be to get dressed every morning and get over to a conference that would be the only time I would see my colleagues all year. I needed to be certain I could put my best foot forward, so I stayed in a timeshare and put the Halfloaf and the Expedition into storage.

Both went into storage because the four-wheel drive Expedition has the strange problem that it is seven feet two inches tall. Many older parking garages are marked for seven feet tall passage, though the warning bar is usually well over the additional two inches. Still, I'm very careful in parking garages. The conference was at an older hotel with an older parking garage and required valet parking. I wasn't about to take any chances, so I got a rental car to use for the week of the conference.

But the rental car was where things really went downhill. The rental agency gave me a free upgrade to a flashy car with New Jersey plates. Right after leaving the office, the car signaled that it needed air in the tires. The office had closed for the day as I was leaving, so I couldn't go back. I stopped at a gas station and filled the tires.

One of my concerns about moving into the RV was how much more I would be out in public and what kind of risks that created with law enforcement. Now I was driving around in this flashy car with problem tires.

In preparation for my new level of risk, I fished the decade-expired bottle of Xanax out of the bottom of my purse and threw it away. I put my car and RV registration on top of the documents in my glove box. I considered getting a dash cam. The dash cam turns out to be what I really needed, though even if I had owned one, I doubt I would have moved it to the rental car.

As I was driving to do a chore the next morning, the rental car alarmed that one of my tires was at 40 percent pressure. I drove carefully down the right lane, looking down the streets to the right for a gas station. Since it had taken several hours to get to 40 percent, my hope was that I could refill it and get back to the rental place to exchange the car. I didn't want to get into a situation where I would be waiting beside the road in the heat, and in any case, there wasn't a spot to pull off.

Finally, I arrived at a corner where the right lane ended as a right turn lane. I was going to follow it around and see what I could find, but looking up I finally saw what I was looking for: a gas station across the street.

Just then a police car drove into the middle of the intersection as if he were blocking traffic for some reason. The light turned green, but neither the car next to me nor I moved. The officer waved his hand at me in a beckoning motion. The person next to me looked over at me, waiting for me to move so he could go. I thought perhaps the officer could see my flat tire and wanted to help me. I couldn't have been more wrong.

He pulled in behind me at the gas station and as he walked up to the car his agitation was clear. Rage radiated off of him. "WHAT DO YOU THINK YOU ARE DOING?" he screamed. "I have a flat tire," I responded. It was the only thing I would say in the entire engagement. I avoided eye contact and assumed a cowering position so he wouldn't feel threatened. I was dealing with a very dangerous man and my one goal was to avoid escalation.

As he stood at my open door, he screamed at me that I didn't have a flat tire. He screamed about New Jersey. He was from New Jersey, and he had a lot of things to express about the state of New Jersey. His rage seemed like a bottomless well as it poured out of him and echoed off the overhang of the gas station.

He finished by saying, "There's another gas station two miles up the road. Go there." He then spun around on his heel and walked back toward the gas pumps. As I sat there trying to figure out what to do, he chatted with his friend who worked at the station. His rage spent on me, he had transformed back into a man who looked normal and relaxed.

I wasn't sure what would happen if I drove two more miles. Was it safe? I consulted Google and found nothing. I called John, who was at work and didn't answer. I had been ordered to leave, but how could I?

I finally decided to go into the gas station building

and ask for help. The person behind the counter told me that the person I needed to speak to was the guy who was outside chatting with the officer. Well, I certainly wasn't going over there!

I stood outside by the front door and waited patiently. Eventually the man gestured for me to walk over. This was not going well at all. I walked over, pretending the officer wasn't there. I did, however, take the opportunity to make a mental note of the officer's license plate number. When I made my complaint, it took a while to track down who the officer was because it turned out he actually worked in a city several miles away.

So, there we were, the gas station worker, the officer I was pretending didn't exist, and me, standing behind the patrol car. "I have a flat tire," I said, building a brick wall in my mind between the officer and me, as I contradicted his assessment of my tire. "I've been told there is a gas station two miles away," I said, as if the person who had told me that wasn't standing right next to me. "The tire is at 40 percent and what I need to know is if it is safe to drive two miles."

"Bring it over here," the gas station worker said. He filled the tire for me. I gave him some cash and I looped behind the gas station building, away from the officer, to leave. The road I arrived at had a "no left turn" sign. The only legal option was to turn right, passing by the officer again. I turned left.

I raised my own voice a bit when I turned the car back in, still shaking with adrenalin and swallowed humiliation. It had a low tire when they had given it to me and sending me out with a bad tire had started this whole chain of events. If they had just given me a regular car, in good repair, none of this would have happened.

They asked if a free day might somehow turn this into a five-star experience. I said that a plain car with a Florida plate would improve the situation greatly. I didn't drive in the direction of that city where the officer didn't work nor the city down the highway where he did for the rest of the week. I will never drive there.

When I filed my complaint in the municipality where this occurred, a supervisor called me to make it very clear that it had not been one of their officers, and it would never be one of their officers. They forwarded the complaint to the other city.

Eventually I spoke with the correct supervisor, who happened to be from New Jersey. He also had a lot to share with me about New Jersey. He apparently could just feel that the woman on the phone, me, wanted to know more about his fascinating career, which included working in New Jersey. I had to listen nicely if I wanted to have a turn to speak.

It turned out that the officer had placed his car in the intersection because he somehow intuited I was going to drive from the right lane into the gas station. He wanted to make sure I didn't get there and had pulled into the intersection to block my path. He had made no gestures. He had screamed at no person.

In fact, he had never been observed showing

hostility to anyone ever. I suggested that perhaps the right way to interact with the public was to write a ticket or to help them. Oh, no need to write a ticket, I was told. It was completely appropriate to just have a calm chat after, I was told in these exact words, I caused him to "fear for his life."

I circumnavigated around the area for the rest of the week. Aside from the destruction that filled the streets with debris, the conference went well. I collected the Expedition and the Halfloaf and headed home.

It was cooler in North Carolina than when I left, and one cold morning a bird tucked itself under the tongue of my trailer and died. In that moment the death of the bird was terrible and meaningless, and in the days before a momentous trip that would completely change my life forever, it seemed a very bad omen. I wrapped up the bird in a plastic bag and threw it in the dumpster.

The conference I had just attended had been built from nothing by a tremendously dynamic woman, Christine Pierre. Out of sheer will, she had created a nonprofit that brought the people in my industry together in a way they never had been before. By the next year she would be dead. Through seemingly good fortune, a tiny spot had been found in her eye when it was less than a millimeter wide. It was destroyed and irradiated for good measure, but it would come back and grow and grow until it killed her.

I wanted the world to stand still when I sold my house. I was so tired. But people and animals would continue to come and go through my life, and through life itself, in an exhausting whirl. Some of our interactions would be destructive, some would be meaningless, and some will stick with me forever.

CHAPTER 7

CHAPTER 7

A Tour of North Carolina

FOR SOME REASON MANY FULL-TIME RVERS insist on framing the rapid touring they did when they first got an RV as a mistake rather than as what they wanted to do at the time. What I wanted to do when I got back to North Carolina was to see my friends. I had obtained this magical suitcase that I could step inside of and bring with me. Why wouldn't I make use of it?

First, I picked up Happy from John's house. I didn't realize the bowl I had purchased for my oatmeal wasn't microwavable. Unfortunately, it also wasn't suitable for Happy to drink from. I had one other bowl that

Happy could drink from, but it was also the bowl I had ended up using for my oatmeal. So, for the first few weeks, each morning I cleaned Happy's water dish, ate my oatmeal, and then cleaned it again and gave it back to him. This is how I earned my merit badge in minimalism.

After I had purchased a more socially acceptable number of appropriate bowls (one for a human and one for a bunny), I headed to the coast. My friend Pam lived out there, and I had not seen her in a long time. She lived in a beautiful oceanfront golf course community. It was exactly the kind of place that would have an HOA that banned RVs, except it was built before people had thought of such things. I squeezed the Halfloaf onto her driveway and tried to make myself as inconspicuous as possible. Even without an HOA, someone might call the police.

This was where I started to realize some of the benefits of having an Airstream. The neighbors did not call the police, as neighbors of people living in RVs often do. Instead they walked their dog around the block a second time to get another look. They asked for tours. They loved the Airstream.

After finishing out the work week, we piled into the Expedition and headed for the Outer Banks. You could practically throw a rock at them from her house, but it was a four-hour drive to take the Halfloaf around on land. I was about to have my first houseguest in my 16-foot house!

Pam was the perfect houseguest. Happy, who is very selective about whom he likes and very clear on whom he doesn't, thought she was great. The resort RV park where we stayed was nearly empty, it being well past the season, but the weather was perfect. I had selected a luxury space with a concrete patio and outdoor furniture. We did all of our cooking outside and watched the only movie I have ever played on the trailer's entertainment system.

When I am staying alone, I shower in the wet bath, but with two people, we used the resort showers. RV park showers are often pretty grim. At this RV park, the showers were tiled with something that looked like marble and were absolutely beautiful.

We went to the Cape Hatteras lighthouse, and I bought a *Passport to Your National Parks.* Most national park visitor centers have an ink stamp for the book. I had had one when I was a child, but the program was just starting then and not every location had the stamps.

Now the stamps are an institution. Certain people will drive far out of their way even when there is no time to actually visit a national park just to get the stamp. Later in the year, I visited Chimney Rock National Monument. It didn't have a visitor center, but it did have a booth staffed by volunteers with their own stamp. The volunteers were there to protect the artifacts and provide interpretive tours. And to make sure my drive was worth it.

Back at the Outer Banks, we ate hamburgers and ice cream. We had the loveliest time. And Pam is probably the last houseguest I will ever have.

First, the dinette (my office) that turned into a bed is now half disassembled to allow for my Herman Miller chair. Second, everything was new and perfectly clean then. Later in the year I actually visited a very proper Japanese woman named Yoshiko, who is a sort of distant grandmother to me (our families have been in touch for over five generations), and I cleaned like mad, certain my house was not to Japanese grandmother standards. Yoshiko was very polite and loved the Airstream, but I doubt anyone would want to stay in my trailer, no matter what their housekeeping standards.

Anyway, back to the Outer Banks. After visiting Pam, I headed to Research Triangle Park to stay at Jordan Lake State Park. This park is at the nexus of the region and only a few minutes from John's house, but I hadn't been there in years.

At Jordan Lake, I backed into my little space on my first try. I looked around to see if anyone was watching, but of course they weren't. Usually the spaces at Jordan Lake aren't little, but this particular one was more suited to a tent than an RV. Under the deep forest canopy, it was dark inside all day long with the water of the lake sparkling a couple hundred yards away.

In the off-season, Jordan Lake has a ridiculously early and uncertain curfew. The sign says one thing, but the staff may keep the gate open an hour later than that. Or they may not, who knows. It's best to get back by the time on the sign or you might get locked out. It's a long walk from the front gate to the campground, and it's a walk that every full-time RVer I know in North Carolina has made.

The sites at Jordan Lake have water but no sewer. My fresh water tank is almost exactly the same size as my sewage tank, so a water connection without a sewer connection is of no use to me. I don't even hook up because if I did fill the water tank without emptying the sewer tank, I would be overweight. I might be able to get a little more use by adding some water, but by knowing exactly how many gallons are on board as they go from one tank to the other, I have a pretty good handle on my total weight. Being overweight can damage the axle. It's also illegal and can void your insurance in an accident.

Ah, you cleverly ask, but what about the solid matter you add to the sewer? This entire project has taught me a lot about that subject actually. Between the water that Happy uses and deposits in his litter box, and the water that I sweat off, I usually lighten my tank load, even with the addition of solid matter, by about 15 percent as it transfers from the fresh tank to the sewer tank.

Leaving Jordan Lake, I found a beautiful dump station and took full advantage of it. The dump station is right by a main road through the park, and earlier I had seen someone with a Cruise America RV appear to be struggling with the dump process. Cruise America is a commonly seen brand of rental RV, either the most popular or just the one with the largest branding on their rigs. You see them everywhere.

I circled back to help the guy. Only a moment had passed, but there were three other people already there. Truly, RVers are always ready to help. And RVers talk about sewage an awful lot. Your tank levels are always on your mind, and somehow that spills into whatever the conversation is. In fact, a woman named Liz Wilcox published a wildly popular e-book, *Tales from the Black Tank,* aimed to "crush any of those #rvlife dreams you've concocted." I assume your RV dreams don't involve sewage.

Visiting my friends from Research Triangle Park, I had to do my best to keep a lid on the sewage talk. They didn't know where the RV park was at Jordan Lake and didn't come out to my house. Plus, at this point a lot of my network still didn't know I was living in an RV. As I transitioned back and forth between the "normal" world of permanently built structures and my little RV in the woods, the two parts of my life became more estranged rather than less. I have not been able to knit them back together.

Before leaving for the winter, I made one final visit to someone whose living situation was a bit more similar to my own. Lucas had been raised in downtown Raleigh by a powerhouse of a single mother who was a local radio DJ and celebrity. He was a successful sales executive in the telecommunications industry. We had met when we were assigned to the same team in MBA school.

Lucas had married an equally dynamic woman

who is a veterinarian and an equestrian. Together, they moved to a rural North Carolina horse farm. Between caring for their flock of chickens and chewing the fat with the fence neighbor, Lucas has continued his career from his home office. Although their house is beautiful, the only local dining-out option is the Waffle House. And his business associates probably aren't interested in the details of mucking out the stalls or ensuring the ground is groomed properly for an expensive show horse.

Like me, Lucas lives between two worlds that exist inside the one state of North Carolina. And like me, he has as much of one world inside him as the other.

CHAPTER 8

Thousand Trails

WHILE I WAS WANDERING AROUND NORTH
Carolina, I started to familiarize myself with my secret
weapon for affordable full-time RV living: Thousand
Trails. Thousand Trails is a network of RV parks accessible for a yearly fee, mostly along the east and west coasts
and in Texas. There are certain circumstances that may
lead to additional daily rates, but for the most part for a
smaller trailer with just one air conditioner (a trailer that
uses a 30-amp power plug instead of a 50-amp power
plug), the daily rate is free.

There are a lot of footnotes and variations, but

in short, Thousand Trails comes in two flavors that full-time RVers would be interested in. One allows you to stay at a Thousand Trails park for two weeks and then be gone for one week. Rinse and repeat as much as you want. The other level allows you to stay for three weeks and then you can go straight to another Thousand Trails park.

Thousand Trails also has an association with some other parks, including an entire other network system available to their top-level members. I have the two-week level as well as the "Parks Collection" which provides access to the Encore chain of parks under the two-week terms. Encore parks saved my bacon when I went to "no parking" California where I could only stay at very expensive RV parks. I stayed at two very desirable Encore parks, Pacific Dunes Ranch and RV Resort in Pismo Beach and San Francisco RV Resort in Pacifica. They required a $20 a day fee, but they were still far cheaper than any other option in the region.

The park where I stay for the winter in Florida is also an Encore, and I have to pay cash because I stay longer than two weeks. The discount I get for my winter stay because I'm a Thousand Trails member completely offsets what my Thousand Trails membership costs. When I add up what living in an RV costs me, I consider my Thousand Trails membership to be free.

Meanwhile, back in North Carolina I was staying at Forest Lake in the unincorporated area of Advance. If you've never heard of Advance that's okay, no one in

North Carolina has either. It was once in the middle of nowhere, but it is rapidly becoming squeezed between the metropolitan areas of Winston-Salem and Charlotte.

I can get just about anything I want while I am in Advance, as long as I'm willing to drive 30 minutes to civilization. This is more typical of Thousand Trails parks than an oceanfront space by the Golden Gate. There's a reason they're affordable.

In fact, I find this isolation makes all of life more affordable. It's harder to spend money. There are no Joneses to keep up with. I spend a lot less money when I'm out here in Advance. I've also been able to develop some ties to the community.

Because there aren't a lot of Thousand Trails parks, over time you start to see the same people again. And even if you've never met someone before, you've stayed at the same places and may know some of the same people. The Thousand Trails Facebook group is about as bad as any other neighborhood Facebook group and I avoid it, but on social media I keep a loose set of connections with people I've met at the parks.

Forest Lake has a small population of long-term sites. When I come back, I try to stay in the same section of the park, so I have come to know my neighbors. One time I was discussing with a neighbor a $2,000 thing I needed to purchase because he happened to own the same thing. When I came back to the park on the next two-week rotation, he had replaced his and offered his old one to me for free.

It touched my heart enormously to have become a member of a community that would foster such thoughtfulness and generosity. The offered part was from an elderly gentleman with whom I had bonded over how some of the limitations of my illness matched those he had acquired through old age. It turned out that his older item wouldn't work out for me, but who among my neighbors in HOA-land would ever have offered me such a gift?

CHAPTER 9

Hitches Are for Girls

THERE'S A RUMOR THAT WOMEN DON'T BUY travel trailers because they are afraid of hitches. I have no idea if it's true. RV salesmen surely have no idea what women RVers think because most of them have never seen one. On the RV sales floor, women are completely invisible.

The one time I went to a small RV show, I had to ask an RV salesman to move out of the way so I could walk into the RV he was trying to sell. In the entire show, not a single salesman spoke to me. The salesman who sold me my Airstream has a few choice words to say about this phenomenon, but he keeps his lips sealed since his miraculous ability to see women brings home the sales commissions.

I hadn't had any thoughts about my hitch one way or the other. If I had purchased something other than a travel trailer, I still would have had to hitch up a car behind it. Hitches are just part of the deal. At first, I did not get along well with mine. As I rushed down to Florida, one part of my hitch seized up. Except for the first night when the employee at the KOA helped me unhitch, I pulled the Halfloaf everywhere I went for three weeks until I returned to Raleigh. At one point along the way, I did stop at the service department of an RV mega-store to see what they could do for me. The guy looked at me, a middle-aged woman, and told me that what I needed to do was "man-handle it more."

Men love to tell me that what I need to do is "man-handle it more," but if they actually do it themselves, they always pick up a tool. One time when my hitch wouldn't latch, a man told me to "man-handle it more" and then walked over and smacked it with a metal bar. I've since learned to bounce the car forward an inch to bump it closed.

John used a screwdriver to work loose a spring that was stuck in my hitching system. He sprayed in silicone lubricant and worked the silicone into the spring until it moved smoothly. Then he gave me the can of silicone, which has been one of the most useful things I own. As the old saying goes, if it moves and it shouldn't, use duct tape. If it doesn't move and it should, well, the saying is to use WD-40. But on an RV, dirt will stick to it and make things worse, so use silicone.

The next week a woman pulled in next to me for her first night in her new RV. She asked me for my top tip for a solo woman RVer. I told her I was brand new and didn't have an answer to that yet. Later in the evening she couldn't get unhitched. I heard the problem before I saw it as the sound of screeching metal cut through the cool dusk, followed by the sound of her pounding on her hitch with a rock. I remembered that actually I did know the answer to her question and gave her my bottle of silicone spray.

CHAPTER 10

The Shooting

IN THE MIDST OF GOING BACK AND FORTH between South Florida and North Carolina, I spent the night at an RV park outside Orlando and someone was shot in the RV next to me.

I was tired so I had gone to sleep around eight p.m. When I woke up a couple of hours later to use the toilet, I could see red, white, and blue lights flashing through a crack in my window shade. Though the lights matched the pattern of police lights, I couldn't imagine why the police would be there. I assumed it was decorations on someone's house and went back to sleep.

I woke up again around four a.m., and the lights were still there. I couldn't think of anything that would keep the police there for six hours, so I was certain I was seeing decorations. The minute I stepped out of my RV in the morning, my across-the-way neighbor was at my door saying, "Hey, did you see all the police cars last night?" No. "Did you hear all the news helicopters?" Nope.

RV air conditioners are ridiculously loud. In higher-end, newer RVs, including Airstreams above the Sport line, you can get ducted air conditioners. In this set-up, the air conditioner is on top of the RV and the air goes into ducts contained in an additional space between the ceiling and the roof. In my RV, the ceiling and roof are sandwiched tightly together and the air conditioner is on the outside, connected directly to the inside with nothing to muffle the sound. Think how loud the air conditioner outside your house is.

My illness causes noise sensitivity and sometimes this is a problem for me with the air conditioner, especially the first time I use it after it has been off for a while. I carry ear plugs and ear muffs that I use when I need to dampen sounds such as the air conditioner noise. When I became noise-sensitive, I headed over to the Autism chat forums for the best advice on what to buy, and the products they recommended among themselves were what I purchased.

That night I wasn't using any of those devices. It was the air conditioner that was louder than the gun shot next door.

When I wrote about the shooting online, my readers did not put themselves in my place. They did not spend the night isolated by the whir of the air conditioner. They did not see the lights. They did not emerge in the morning to shocked neighbors.

Instead, they had their own story to tell. The story rolled over what anyone who was there actually experienced. Whoever had been shot should have had a gun. No one should have a gun. This is why I carry a gun. This is why you are nuts to carry a gun. One of the gun owners explained to me that he doesn't let his perception of crime levels affect where he stays, because he has a gun. However, he doesn't "let" his wife go out alone in places where there is crime.

That I traveled alone, that I might not have a gun, that I was not the person who was shot was a profound disappointment to him. My unaffectedness, my survival, was an affront not only to his gun ownership but to the structure of his marriage.

As soon as I told my story, it was no longer my own. The distortion of abstractions came at me in a discordant rush just as I was experiencing the concreteness of *life* in a new way. In many ways, this experience would repeat throughout the year. My life in an RV was a story to be told by others, about some other thing.

Just as I was setting out, the book *Nomadland* was making the rounds, a book length version of highjacking the lives of RVers to make points about topics unrelated to their actual experiences. In *Nomadland* the story of RV life is transformed into a story of despair by an author conflicted about the happiness of rainbows (really, it's in the book).

As the author was turning the lives of others into abstractions of her own vision of the world, she was oddly enough abstracting her own real life by pretending to be an author living in an RV as she researched her book even as she was, in fact, *an author living in an RV*. When I read her book, I too was an author living in an RV and writing a book, except I wasn't pretending to be anything else.

I think a lot of people reading my book actually do want to live in an RV. Not just in that they need to know how to sell their house and how to connect their sewer, but that they want to do those things in order to connect with the reality of their own lives. They see themselves becoming the creator of their own story instead of being a part of someone else's.

As loud as the abstract voices can be, most people do want to live their own story. The RV group where this guns and shootings discussion was happening was fairly large and fairly diverse. About a third of Americans own guns, and there is no reason to think the breakdown is any different for RVers. Most people in that group weren't trying to make my story tell their story, they were off living their own story.

As for this end of this story, I say as a person who was there and can recount what happened, it turned out that the child who had been shot in the leg by another child was only slightly wounded. I never found out if the adult who had left a gun within reach of a child was charged. Several weeks later and a few states away, I mentioned the incident and someone said they had heard about it in an RV Facebook group.

CHAPTER 11

Harvest Hosts

ON MY FINAL TRIP SOUTH, THIS TIME TO spend the winter in Miami, I stayed in the parking lot of a farm stand just north of the city. When I got there, I found it was more like a small specialty market. The farm stand was a member of Harvest Hosts, a collection of farm stands, wineries, museums, and the like that will allow self-contained (meaning it has a bathroom built in) RVs to stay one night for free.

On the drive down, I had stayed at another farm that was closed for the season, but the farming family let me stay out in a field. "Normally we come out to say hi," the man had said, "but there's a football game on tonight." They should have charged rent for writers to stay in their field. Out in the bare furrows, I got more work done than I have in any other place.

Later, I would stay at another farm in California. The farmer had been called away, so he left me the combination to the lock on the gate. When I parked on a dirt road beside one of the fields, the children came out to check on me. The next morning when the market opened, I purchased fresh strawberries and ate them there next to the field.

I don't stay a lot at Harvest Hosts. They often have a gate that locks when the business is closed, so you have to be sure you're going to get there on time. Calling on the day of arrival is a little rude, so you have to know where you're going to be a few days ahead of time, which isn't really my style. My illness means that I also have to worry about getting pulled into a farm or winery tour that exceeds my ability to stand after a day of driving.

I was at a farm stand market outside Miami because in the strange pace of dealing with Miami-area traffic, I knew I would be arriving in the afternoon and did not want to go through the traffic to get to the RV park south of Miami where I was going to spend the winter.

The farm stand had homemade ravioli with stuffing mixtures that sounded fantastic. I purchased one to eat that night and another to have when I arrived in Miami. A few weeks later I opened my freezer and found the one hidden away.

I had parked at the back of the parking lot over-looking a lush field. As I prepared my ravioli dinner, the farm workers tended to the field outside my door. By the time I was ready for bed, it seemed like no one was around, but I occasionally heard the sound of machinery turning on and then off. I locked my front door and got into bed, uncertain who was still out there.

In the morning I realized that the sound had been a generator on a refrigerated truck cycling on and off. Despite the slightly disquieting night, having breakfast while I watched a tractor making passes through the field in the morning mist was the perfect end to my fall wandering.

CHAPTER 12

Winter in Miami

BEING ABLE TO WINTER IN MIAMI WAS THE entire reason I was living in the RV in the first place. My symptoms tend to worsen considerably for about six weeks before and after the solstice. The previous few years had felt like I was enduring some sort of medieval curse as my life was controlled by the solstice. Traveling from North Carolina to Miami offered a chance of a cure, but it was not a guarantee. Depending on which research numbers were used and what category of seasonal affective disorder I fit into, there was a 15 to 30 percent chance that it wouldn't work at all.

Fortunately for me, it was a cure, and the winter passed as if it were just more summer. Aside from one brief cool snap that found the full-time residents of the park hastily servicing their furnaces, it was hot enough that I had to run my air conditioner every afternoon.

I would start the day with my door open, eating my breakfast and drinking my tea in the natural air. Toward noon, I would close the door and switch on the air conditioner. In the late evening, I would visit the hot tub and by the time I returned to the Halfloaf, it would be time to turn off the air conditioner for the night.

Because I was staying at a monthly rate, I also had to pay for electricity. I had heard horror stories about $500 electric bills and part of the reason I limited my air conditioner use was in anticipation of the electricity bill. I need not have worried about it. I'm one-fourth the size of the RVs that many people use for long-term stays, and I only have one air conditioner instead of their two or three. Even at the RV park's mark-up rate, my electricity bill was less than it had been in my house.

Miami was one of my favorite cities from my road warrior days, which was part of why I had chosen this spot in Southern Florida. At my old job, my employer allowed me to fly anywhere for the weekend as long as it cost the same or less than it cost to fly home. Direct flights to Miami in the off season weren't very expensive, and I had a close friend in the city. I had been a regular visitor.

This new living situation was a bit more

frustrating. It was nearly a 45-minute drive to South Beach, and once I got there, what was I going to do? Visiting one place to eat and driving all the way back wasn't worth the trouble. I could no longer walk around for an enjoyable afternoon. Also, half of what I owned was in my car, and I was leery of parking it downtown.

The Miami Zoo and some other attractions were closer, but even a couple of years earlier visiting the zoo had been a struggle. I have never seen whatever was beyond the snack stand in the middle of the property. With my illness, I simply can't walk that far and be certain I can get back to my car and be well enough to drive home.

I went to a few restaurants in Homestead, and they had their own character. Homestead wasn't bad, but it wasn't the glitter of Miami. Eventually, I stumbled across an open-air ceviche restaurant and bar that wasn't so far away. They played Latin music and a body of water was in view. Being there felt good, and the amount of foot traffic in the open parking lot felt safe. It soon became my place where everybody knows your name.

I found that Key Largo was easier to get to than South Beach, at least when driving mid-week. In Key Largo, I could have lunch on a patio overlooking the water. My friend and I took a boat tour of Everglades National Park.

Some things about the RV park community didn't match where I was in life. Living around healthy retirees, some of whom had been on permanent vacation for more than a decade, was a little hard to take. As nice as most RVers are, many can be a little tone deaf about how fast the world is changing around them as they revel in their days as the last American pensioners.

Fortunately, my daily patterns put me more in contact with the working residents of the park. My site was odd in that my front door faced the front door of my neighbor, a divorced waiter whose grown children visited from time to time.

Also, I learned how popular RV rentals are with European tourists. In Miami, RVs with the names of various rental agencies emblazoned on the sides brought Scandinavians, Germans, French, and more. The space directly behind me was for short-term visitors, and all of Europe was represented by the end of the winter. One week would be techno pop blaring at midnight. The next would be thoughtful conversations about American apartheid around the hot tub.

Staying in one spot for so long had some elements of restfulness to it, but it was countered by the stresses of life. You start to think of chores you might do next week, of cycles of activities you must continue. Without a regular pack-up, the house became cluttered. It wasn't the RV life I had experienced in the weeks before.

CHAPTER 13

Finding the New Me

FOR SIX MONTHS I LOST MYSELF. AS I SOLD my house and moved into the Halfloaf, I had floated on a set of chores and driving to the conference, to my friends' homes, and then all the way back to Florida. I had been advised not to tell business associates right away that I lived in an RV. That strange isolation was part of the disconnect that left me feeling adrift.

The idea behind the delay in telling business associates was that they would see that work had been getting done the same as always, and they wouldn't be concerned about the new arrangement. My social life and my work life are heavily entwined, so this decision meant I couldn't post anything on social media and couldn't tell most of my friends what I was doing. In any case, the reaction from the first few people I did tell left me less than eager to tell anyone else.

I arbitrarily set my arrival in Florida as the date to announce where I was living. When I actually made the announcement, only one of my clients was tied closely enough to my personal social media to see it. Choosing this timing to prove that work had been going great while I was living in the RV didn't turn out so well. Between a respiratory infection and some other issues that had nothing to do with the RV, work had actually suffered.

Before I moved into the RV, one of my largest clients and I had decided to part ways at the end of the year, and I found myself uncertain how I was going to pay all of my employees in January. I had hoped that one would quit and solve the problem for me, and that's exactly what happened. The person who quit was one of my most consequential employees, and therefore one of the most expensive. While that solved my financial problem, I was suddenly thrust into a different rhythm of work as the one client left and I was picking up the tasks of the former employee.

The months in Miami did turn out to be good for showing that RVing would not be a distraction. Sitting in the same spot for two months meant there wasn't too much else to say about it. RVing didn't dominate my life the way it had the first couple of months. I never did get around to telling some of my clients where I live, and then as time went on it became more and more of an odd thing to bring up. They never talk about where they live, so maybe it is not so strange that I don't talk about where I live. To this day some people still aren't quite sure where I live, and I haven't clarified the issue. I think some of my professional connections think I live in AirBnBs.

A lot of people talk about struggling to adapt to their first year in an RV. It's common to tell new RVers that they should stick it out for 12 months so they can get to the part where they will enjoy it. That didn't happen to me. It never occurred to me not to like living in an RV. It wasn't really a choice; it was just a fact. None of that occupied me and now, sitting for two months, my mind grew restless.

That's nothing new. I've always been a restless person. Part of the reason I started a business was because I was bored. I didn't want to spend the rest of my life doing something I already knew how to do. I wanted to do something I didn't know how to do, which is what I did with my communications company.

The secret I had tapped into is that most people have the ability to become better at one thing than anyone else. Malcolm Gladwell is famous for the theory that it takes practice. But it takes more than that. It takes focus. And it also takes some innate ability. This idea is discussed in the book *Now, Discover Your Strengths* by Marcus Buckingham and Donald O. Clifton.

To turn a strength into a viable career or business, practice on yourself and your friends. You can even
practice on a paying customer who will receive a great
rate in return for being your guinea pig. If you show
competence and confidence, that will happen. And then
you've got experience, and then you become an expert.
I've run my entire career this way. I have a degree in
philosophy, and I work in biotechnology. Someday I'll
tell that whole story.

Having work was a problem I had solved. Having
a place to live that worked with my illness was a problem I had solved. The problem that had been pushed onto
the back burner was "Who am I now?"

I'm someone whose personality is to engage a
lot. Over my life, I've held several demanding volunteer positions in addition to my work. That's not a thing
I can do any more. My physical circumstances suggest
a move toward a contemplative life. An RV could be a
mini-monastery. But would that fit me?

In the spring before I moved into my RV, I had
visited the Abbey of St. Walburga in Colorado. The
Benedictine nuns who live at the Abbey attend chapel
five times a day in traditional habits, then change back
into jeans and run a working cattle ranch. They have
work, contemplation, and hospitality. Over my first year
living in the Airstream, I worked my way through *Benedict's Rule: A Translation and Commentary* by Terrence
G. Kardong, trying to find my footing.

At the time Benedict was writing, some people

who wanted to find God left their communities and embarked on a private journey. They would go into the desert or have themselves built into the wall of a church. Benedict had done this himself. He eventually came to be seen as a teacher, and people went out into the desert and imposed themselves on his private journey. How could he transform what he had found into a new kind of community life? He wasn't the first to face this problem—his *Rule* is largely cribbed from someone else—but his development of a response to the challenge has been the most enduring.

Then, as now, the balance of privacy and community is vital to Christian living. Benedict's focus on hospitality brings that balance into harmony. You have a private space, and yet people are welcomed within it.

Living in an RV creates an odd situation where you have both more privacy and less privacy. Sometimes you can feel completely unmoored, like you have too much privacy and are unknown to anyone. Other times it can seem impossible to have any privacy at all.

When I first moved into the thin shell of my RV and spent the night in a parking lot, taking off my clothes and taking a shower in the middle of the parking lot was difficult. That's no longer a problem, but your neighbors can come to know quite a lot about you quite quickly. Just by standing near your RV, they can know if you're taking a shower or having a conversation on the phone or snoring.

On the other hand, sometimes you can go a month

or more without having a face-to-face conversation with anyone who really knows you. At the same time you crave making connections, you have to protect your own sphere of legitimate privacy. In any case, the barista at Starbucks probably doesn't want to know your life story.

Online, I started a conversation about privacy with people who work and live in RVs. I immediately got some very passionate replies about making authenticity primary. Keeping anything private, some felt, impinged on their authenticity. They had moved away from normal society to get away from that very limitation.

After everything I had been through, these replies didn't match my experience. Women face a particular problem with privacy in that they are often seen as public property. People with disabilities face prejudice, and then when they respond to that by erecting some privacy around how they manage their lives, they're scolded for inauthenticity. What is more authentic than protecting your soul and your ability to make enough money to eat and have shelter?

This conversation reminded me that privacy is not only a tactic for managing my life but also an essential part of humanity. With no private life, there is no public life. This is a foundational concept in modern democracy, but it is also as ancient as Benedict's attempt with his rule.

The challenge I was facing in finding that balance wasn't just the RV but also in the very difficult times in which we live. There are a lot of difficult things, but one that I face in particular in these times and in my RV life is how to deal with people who use white supremacist symbols. This puzzle is something that really challenges the core values about hospitality that I have learned from Benedict and Benedictine thought. The very nature of these symbols is to make some people in our community know they are unwelcome. What is my proper place in how welcoming I am to those who use them? Later in this book I'll tell a specific story about this challenge.

Near the end of my first year living in the Halfloaf, I was feeling that I wasn't drawing any closer to God. Yet in some ways I was without even realizing it. Simply by detaching myself from the sticky web of suburban living, I've had more space to allow God to rise in the values that shape my life. Publishing this book, some truths of which I was afraid to say in my old life, is one part of that. Learning to turn off the noise of the world long enough to even write a book is a step toward the kind of thoughtful and present person I want to be. I haven't perfected privacy, but I've gotten more out of privacy than I ever did before.

Though I've found a much better community than I did in suburbia, I'm not sure I've really found my community yet. I have plenty of friends, but everything about how I interact with people seems disjointed, per-haps even more disjointed than it was when I lived in a house. I engage with everyone in part—an RV person, a biotechnology person, a philosophy person, a theology person—but there's not much continuity and few people known to me are known to each other. Hospitality, rather than being a habit, is something that has to be invented anew for each relationship and each situation. This is perhaps a problem of twenty-first century life that even living in an RV can't solve.

As I was trying to sort this out, winter was coming to an end. It was time to head west, first to attend a conference of full time RVers in Texas and then to visit my family in California.

CHAPTER 14

The Atchafalaya River and the Real America

ON MY DRIVE WEST TOWARD TEXAS, ONE OF my stops was the Atchafalaya National Heritage Area Welcome Center. I hadn't meant to spend the night there. Through Louisiana, I-10 is one long bridge across a swamp. One of the few off-ramps is the welcome center, and I stopped there to research where I was going to spend the night. As I pulled into the parking lot, I noticed an absence of "no parking" signs. A look at my Allstays app quickly confirmed that parking was allowed.

I went inside to sign in and learned that not only

was parking allowed, but a security guard sat in a booth all night to keep an eye on us, and there was free coffee in the morning. They also gave me a sticker for my scrapbook.

I walked through the little museum, but I wanted to find out more. I returned to the Halfloaf and started an online search for information. It turns out that the story is a microcosm of exactly what the "real America" is and why I had missed so much of it in my five years with a job as a road warrior. Is the real America found in the cities? Or is it found in the dying towns the Westward Migration left dotted across the country?

Where a person finds the real America perhaps says more about them than about whatever is real. And wherever one thinks they are going to find the real America, and whatever history supports that ideal, the Atchafalaya River is a comeuppance that is both absurd and horrifying.

The river used to be almost entirely jammed with logs. The local indigenous people saw this as a gift that meant raiding peoples couldn't sneak down the river and attack them. Captain Henry Shreve saw the logs as an impediment to trade. In the 1830s, he opened up the river and also changed its course. A part of the river system crowded with logs again, and he opened it up again.

By the 1860s, water that had been flowing down the Mississippi River began to divert into the Atchafa-laya. Despite millions spent since then to keep water in the Mississippi, the amount diverting to the Atchafalaya has continued to increase. At some point in the future, perhaps after a great flood or hurricane damages the containment system, the Mississippi will completely divert to the Atchafalaya.

In one fell swoop, river access to the ports of Baton Rouge and New Orleans will end. The Port of New Orleans in combination with the Port of South Louisiana is one of the top ten ports by volume in the world. The blow will shake the economy of the entire world.

My old job took me to the hustle and bustle of New Orleans. My new RV took me to this quiet swamp that will someday shake the thrones of faraway kings. When "real RVers" (more on this in the next chapter) admonish us to see the "real America," I wonder what that means. Is the real America this swamp that will be the ultimate revenge on the sprawling global economy that invaded and attempted to remake it?

Or is the "real America" a dying rural town founded by those long-ago pioneers? What makes a dying rural town more "real" than successful cities, big and small, connected by America's interstates and housing the bulk of our latest immigrants? I have visited these towns and, where English is an option, spoken with some of their residents.

Many of them have a fluid relationship with those cities. Even people who are "from here" have rarely lived entirely "here," or identify with just that one plot of land. This is even true of the town where I was born and where my father still has a cattle ranch. The river that starts in quiet farmland is the same river that rushes through the bustling port. Nature is always connected to what is down the road.

The realness of these towns, their actual lived existence, is intimately tied with the modern cities that a real RVer eschews. In fact, they are a very part of that tapestry of woven lives across the continent. This is, in a way, the life I have come to lead as I slip into Research Triangle Park and then back out again to the rural parts of North Carolina and the nation.

Meanwhile, there is the realness of nature. Of a river that returned an attempt to tame it with a guarantee of catastrophe. Of the strange landscape of New Mexico and the mountains of Colorado that I would later encounter.

When I thought I had been encountering all of America with my previous job, I had actually just been following the rivers of commerce. The Atchafalaya proved that those human rivers, which seemed like solid moorings, are in reality only temporary waypoints. The real structure of America is the actual moorings that make up the land. This structure was something I had not seen clearly since I left the cattle ranch of my childhood. Seeing it across America was something I had yet to experience. Coming back to that real structure would change me.

In the flow of commerce, in the mathematics of the city, I am a person with a disability. If a job is to pick up a rock, I am not an economically viable solution for that job because I cannot pick up a rock. This is one reality of my life. But there is another reality that exists at the same time. In nature, I pick up a rock. It is millions of years old. There is no urgency. What is my job even for? In nature, I am a person not an economic unit.

When I was growing up on a rural cattle ranch, we always talked about "ranch time." It's something I experience whenever I go back. As the town is left behind and the miles close in on the ranch, time becomes an *Alice in Wonderland* experience. It isn't what you expect it to be; it isn't what it was when you were in town just a moment ago.

Over the last year, I have learned that this is the pace of the ancient moorings of the land. You can't be on the clock in the forest. The clock is not made for this place. The clock is certainly not made for the Atchafalaya River.

CHAPTER 15

Am I a Real RVer Yet?

IN TEXAS, I CAME FACE-TO-FACE WITH A "real RVer" in a gathering of mostly full-time RVers. I sat down to dinner with two other couples I had not met before, and I casually asked one of the couples where they were from. "We hate that question," the man exclaimed forcefully. "We wrote a blog post about how much we hate that question."

How pompous can you get? You wrote a blog post? Half the people at the event were bloggers. "It's that we live in an RV," his wife clarified. Pretty much everyone there lived in an RV.

"People never understand that we live in an RV," the guy continued. "They ask us where we're from and when we say we live in an RV, they just don't get it." The woman turned to me and cooed, "You must not be full-time."

I thought about a few of the higher-profile names at the conference who had a home base. I thought about the total transformation of my life that had been required to become a full-time RVer. I wanted to tell these people that they were small-minded and rude, but I didn't want to be that confrontational. It is, after all, a community.

"Oh no, I'm full-time," I said. "It's just that other people are usually…" I searched for a word that said what I meant without being the equivalent of punching her in the face. "Nicer." She giggled out an uncomfortable "I'm sorry" and touched my arm. The conversation at the table continued a little longer, and then I left.

I've been accused of not being a real full-time RVer in a number of different ways over the last year. Being a North Carolina resident is one. I haven't transferred my domicile (my legal address) to Florida, Texas, or South Dakota, the most popular places in the country.

You need to understand that these are things some people in the RVing "community" have no problem saying about people like me. Or saying right to me. A lot is made of the RV community, including by me, but it has its problems just like any other community. In a group that tends to define itself by doing things differently, the shadow of the need to define an in-group and an out-group still lurks over how that definition is shaped.

Specifying an out-group is usually the work of anxiety, and like anxiety, it is self-contradictory. Anxiety tells you that you do too much and you do too little. Consequently, I have been defined "out" for contradictory reasons.

I'm a fake RVer because I have a home base. A place where my business network congregates, where John lives, where Happy's vet is, where all my doctors are, and where my ACA health insurance policy that covers all those doctors requires me to spend some time.

I'm a fake RVer because I live in a small rig. I drive on the freeway if it suits me. I stay at casinos and urban locations if it suits me. When I post pictures on social media, I've been told that real RVers only stay in nature.

I'm a fake RVer because I have a job in which I interact with the normal corporate world and, for me, there is a difference between the week and the weekend.

I'm a fake RVer because I don't share my location online. I have found that the concept of "safety" is used as a weapon against single women RVers. They won't tell us we shouldn't be out here, but they'll tell us we need to be obsessed with our safety. Then if we do take some action for our safety, we don't understand how open real RVers are.

I'm a fake RVer because I spend most of my time in my trailer; I do not "live out of my rig instead of in it."

And I'm a fake RVer because I don't have the ability to manhandle a solution to every problem that comes my way.

Not only can I not change my tire, I can't even lift my spare tire off its cradle. I carry a ladder that I've asked other people to use for me because I can't climb a ladder. I pay for RV washes and repairs that other people would do themselves. I pay what some people like me call the "disability tax."

Remember that the legal definition of an RV is mostly about living in less than 400 square feet. That's what we all have in common. If you live in an RV, you're a full-time RVer. There are no other rules. You don't even have to be able to drive.

Some prig with a Florida plate who wants to vote in a place he refuses to admit he lives doesn't make me feel like a fake RVer, but he doesn't make me feel like I've become a member of any kind of tribe either.

I'm as much a real full-time RVer as anyone else who lives in an RV, and that's a pretty diverse group. Later in the year, in Tahoe, I would have the experience that did make me feel a member of the tribe. And it would be with someone completely different from the people I had just met.

═══════════════

CHAPTER 16

Bad Choices and Bad Advice

SOMEONE WHO ONLY SEES ONE WAY OF doing things isn't a good person to ask for advice. Often, people create an illusion for themselves that there is only one right answer so that they don't have to take responsibility for their choices. This is the person who will tell you with perfect assurance what a "real RVer" does. And they will be wrong. Every time.

It still amazes me when I see people on social media or at a campground explaining to others how impossible it is to live in the RV that I own. In their universe, being full-time required them to purchase the largest coach possible. A person in a coach like that has a completely different experience of living full-time in an RV than I do.

All of our experiences are different. We have different hobbies; we want to see different things. Some people like to travel fast, some people stay months or even years in one place. Being different is fine. There is no need to erase the experiences of people living differ-ent lives in order to validate your own. I got a lot out of the YouTube channels of various full-time RVers, but I didn't expect my life to be the same as any of theirs. My RV life is my own.

As I mentioned, I fell into having an 85-watt solar panel on my roof because the RV available when I was buying already had one. It was the best mistake ever. With a few hours of sun per day, all of the functions of my little trailer work perfectly well off that solar panel and one AGM battery (a kind of lead acid battery that doesn't require water).

To power my computer and my "screen of doom," the largest flatscreen available for sale at the time I bought it, I started out with a 300-watt hour lithium battery. Yes, watt hour. Lithium batteries are measured differently from lead acid batteries, which are measured in amp hours. I was using up the 300 watt hours, so I decided to purchase a 1000-watt hour Goal Zero battery before I left Miami. This was a good choice. I had proven the need for the purchase instead of buying something "pre-need."

But then I made a bad choice. I thought I wanted a 200-watt solar panel from Goal Zero to power the battery. The battery is capable of powering my microwave and Instant Pot, but only if I have a large solar panel to recharge it. When the solar panel I had in mind wasn't hooked up to the Goal Zero battery, I could hook it up to the trailer through a charge controller I put together and perhaps be able to keep the trailer battery charged a little longer on a cloudy day.

There were a lot of problems with this plan. First, I have never once left an off-grid location because of a cloudy day. My solar panel already met my needs for powering the trailer, even on overcast days. If the weather is bad enough that I have to leave an off-grid location because I only have one solar panel, I probably don't want to be at an off-grid location.

Next, the solar panel was so huge that I couldn't get it out of my Expedition without unhitching. And I have never once unhitched when off-grid. Also, I so jealously guard my battery power when I'm off-grid that I don't use my microwave and Instant Pot. The only times I have used them have been when I was spending one night driving to another campground or stopping somewhere for lunch. I don't need a solar panel for that.

I made a mistake when I assumed I would use the solar panels for behaviors that I had not first seen myself having. This is the trouble with "pre-need" buying. At the end of the year, I sold the solar panel to a friend. The lesson was made complete when it was destroyed in shipping, leaving both of us with nothing.

But what if I had asked for advice online? I would have been told that no one could tell me how much power I needed without a power audit and that I needed 200 watts and a lot more. I've seen a 100-watt panel derisively called a "trickle charger," a charger for keeping your battery topped off when your trailer is in storage.

Experts are often the worst people to ask for advice. They revel in the complexities of their field and are likely to give you the most expensive and complicated solution. Even the advice to do an energy audit, while reasonable to save money before doing complicated wiring, is needlessly complicated for simply hooking up a solar panel to a pre-wired system. It's pretty easy: buy one panel. If that's not enough, buy another one.

When you have a specific problem that needs a specific solution, this is the time when it can be best to simply copy what someone else has done. There are plenty of YouTubers who have documented every solution to every problem they have found. I specifically say YouTubers because seeing is believing. Remember the guy in the huge coach that wanted to tell me what it's like to live in my Sport 16? On RV chat forums, there are people who will give you advice who don't even own an RV.

Another example is the important issue of cellular connectivity. There are a lot of cellular data service booster options and there is a fabulous set of experts out there at a site called Technomadia.com who can help you sort through them. I had a cell phone carrier before I left my old house. For my demonstrated need, it's working fine. I copied the booster set up from YouTubers Mortons on the Move. It works fine. If I ever want to get deeper into better solutions, though, I will definitely go to Technomadia.

I just don't have the time or energy to get the best solution in every case. People who do that are called "maximizers." I'm not a maximizer by personality, and it's worked well for dealing with my illness. To clarify the difference between a maximizer and what is sometimes called a "satisfiser," the best example I can give is from when I lived in a house and my dishwasher died.

A maximizer might compare all of the dishwashers on *Consumer Reports* to find the best one. They'll then comb through the prices at area stores. A maximizer will get the best product at the best price every time.

I have a friend who is a high-level executive at a technology company and a committed maximizer. He had a house built for his family, and he personally researched every component down to which brand of light switches to buy. I cannot imagine what this cost in lost opportunities to make more money or spend more time with his family.

When my dishwasher died, I drove a half mile to the closest appliance store. I looked at the four varieties of dishwashers they sold and narrowed my choice to the two of them that had features I liked. While standing in the store, I brought up *Consumer Reports* on my phone and determined which one had the best rating.

I bought that dishwasher. The entire project from learning my dishwasher was unrepairable to owning a new dishwasher took less than 30 minutes.

Hobbyists frequently act as maximizers, even if it isn't their core personality. They want to spend time messing with their RV. They want to buy the brands and models that reflect their personality to their friends and other hobbyists they meet when they go camping.

For some people—and a lot of these people own Airstreams—their RV brand choice is a wealth signifier to themselves and others. Just like cars with run-flat tires that never leave the city, you will meet a hobbyist with 600 watts of solar who never leaves the campground.

There is absolutely nothing wrong with what they are doing. I have hobbies too. I know ridiculous things about fountain pens and fountain pen ink. I have three bottles of pink ink that the average person can't tell apart. If you use a roller-ball on a yellow legal pad at work, my pen knowledge is of no use to you.

But as a full-time RVer whose main concern is having a roof that doesn't leak over my head, the primary interests of RV hobbyists have nothing to do with my needs. Experts and maximizers generally don't match my needs and definitely don't match my available energy. Satisfising means solving the problem and moving on to better things.

CHAPTER 17

A Series of Unfortunate Events in New Mexico

THIS IS GOING TO BE A VERY LONG STORY because there were a lot of unfortunate events in one 24-hour period. I'm going to get to the point right here: There are various functions necessary for survival and you need to have a couple of different ways of accomplishing them all. These include warmth and shelter, food, water, and hygiene. If you want not only to survive but also to be comfortable, all of these require even more attention. In this story I become uncomfortable, but my survival is never in doubt.

I had started the day in the dunes outside Roswell, New Mexico. After spending the night in astonishing winds, I woke up to interior walls coated with sand and a very unhappy rabbit. A tiny dune had grown behind my trailer and even tinier dunes behind each tire.

I drove into Roswell and because my trailer is so small, I was able to stop at the famed Cowboy Café and have breakfast. (Seriously, don't take your trailer there if it is longer than 16 feet and don't assume you'll be able to park there even if it is 16 feet.)

Leaving Roswell, I drove about halfway across the state on back roads and found a little spot in the woods to park. It was actually a ridiculous spot in the woods. To get to it you first had to drive along the top of a levee, and then drive down a ramp built into the side of the levee into the campground.

The campground itself was a bowl of exquisitely dry tinder. A sign said that not even propane stoves were allowed, but I was going to have to run my furnace to stay warm that night. It was in no way safe, and I should have moved on to the Walmart 20 minutes away, but I was feeling just too clever that I had found the spot. I did check multiple times to ensure there was no plant material against the side of trailer near the heat exhausts from the furnace, the water heater, and the refrigerator.

At the entrance to the little park, there was an old sign that was peeling and faded. Aside from the newly added note about the fire risk, none of it was legible. The website was unclear about whether overnight parking was permitted. I had found out about the park because a person had marked it on a website as a place for overnight camping based on a conversation with a ranger from an agency that didn't even manage this park.

As soon as I parked, I got into my bed for a nap. I was woken from my nap by someone knocking on my door. In the woods, I don't answer my door for anyone. This was the first and only time this has happened to me, but I am certain that is my rule. I don't know where this guy came from. There were no other cars around. Eventually, he walked back into the woods, and I was left with a yet stronger sense of unease about the place.

I worked at my computer with my lights out and my windows covered with extra blankets, just to make sure no lights shone through the forest in case I wasn't allowed to stay there. I had stubbornly decided to stay, and I didn't want someone in a uniform knocking on my door next. Finally, it was late enough to try to sleep.

I woke up at about two a.m., freezing cold. I turned the furnace down and then back up. It turned on for a few minutes and then went out again. According to the weather report when I went to sleep, it was 25 degrees outside. It was also the middle of the night, and as we all know, this is when ghosts and goblins get up to their shenanigans. Paranoid RVers sometimes talk about how someone might mess with something outside to lure you out. I decided to freeze until sunrise.

This decision lasted until I was in fact freezing. Happy has a fur coat and is fine down to freezing temperatures. I have no fur coat and hate being cold. My thought was that my first propane tank must have run out and my second one was off. I have a regulator that automatically switches between them, but sometimes I leave the second tank off so I can't empty out both my tanks without knowing it.

Eventually, I ran outside and turned on both tanks and ran back inside and locked the door. The heater came back on for a while, but eventually it went out again. I couldn't sleep in the cold, so I decided to work until sunrise. I wanted to leave, but scrambling up the side of the levee in the dark seemed like a bad idea. If I missed the turn onto the top, I would fall down the other side into the river.

I could have sat in the car and run the engine to keep warm if it had been required for my survival. As my survival wasn't in question, the ghosts and goblins won the night. I stayed in the trailer and shivered.

Finally, the sun came up. I put Happy in the car, and after a few cold turns it started. As I fiddled with my electronics in the cold, I dropped my TPMS (tire pressure monitoring system) and somehow erased the car tires from the screen. I had spent some of my time during the night loading audio books, but they were corrupted and wouldn't play. I hadn't even put the car in drive and already things were going comically wrong.

Now I had to get back on top of the levee. On the ranch where I grew up, my father taught me not to drive in four-wheel drive, telling me, "If you get stuck in four-wheel drive, you're really stuck. But if you get stuck in two-wheel drive, you can use four-wheel drive to get out."

I don't take the Halfloaf anywhere I don't think I have a good chance of getting out of in two-wheel drive. I probably could have scrambled up the side of the levee in two-wheel drive, but then there was the turn at the top and the potential for disaster on the other side. I ignored my father's advice and drove up slowly in four-wheel drive.

Thirty minutes down the road, I stopped at a gas station to fill the tank. When I got back in and turned the key, the car wouldn't start. I carry a lithium car starter, so if this had happened in the woods, I would have been able to start the car. I would have been certain a ghost was going to get me, but I would have been able to start the car.

Here, the owner of the gas station sold me a sandwich made by his wife and jump started my car. He asked me which way I was going and told me there was a garage about 150 miles away that would sell me a new battery. I just needed not to forget I didn't have a battery and turn off the car between here and there.

I have an extended warranty on the car and the RV, but out here neither of those meant a thing. The closest warranty provider for my car was probably in Albuquerque or Flagstaff. Albuquerque meant driving opposite to the way I was headed. Flagstaff required getting on the freeway.

The problem, I quickly learned, was that my car had a feature to make sure I indeed did not forget about the dead battery. That feature was not to go into high gear. I drove across the remainder of New Mexico at 45 miles per hour.

I drove through the Very Large Array. I drove past the turn to White Sands. I drove over a lava flow. I drove through deserts and over wooded hills. Most regrettably, I drove through Pietown, New Mexico, without stopping to get pie.

I didn't remember the name of the town where the man had said I would find a battery, but near the Arizona border, I came upon a repair shop that struck me as the sort of place that might have a battery. I was a little nervous because I was mostly at their mercy, especially after I turned off the car. They quickly replaced the battery and charged me a reasonable price, for which I was very grateful. I sent a thank you letter a few days later.

Down the street, I stopped to fill my propane tanks. It turned out that they were both almost full. Why my furnace had gone out in the middle of the night remained a mystery, but that cause would soon be revealed.

The campground I had found on the map at the beginning of the day was now only about an hour away. I arranged for a site with the campground host, who worked a job in town during the day and ran the campground via text messages. I explained the trouble I was having with my furnace, and she summoned some neighbors who might be able to help.

Meanwhile, I had no way to keep warm inside my trailer. My air conditioner also works as a heat pump if I'm plugged into electricity, but only down to 40 degrees. It was supposed to be another 25-degree night, and I did not want to be cold again. The neighbors weren't available right away, so I started to take the furnace apart myself. Inside I found a small, incinerated snake.

The neighbors arrived, each with an ancient revolver strapped to his hip. When people offer to help, sometimes you just have to go with it. A man once knocked the regulator loose from my propane tank while holding a lit cigarette between his fingers. I stood back and let him.

The pistol-packing neighbors checked the circuit board with a tester and declared it toast. I probably wouldn't be able to get it fixed until I reached California, and until then I had a lot of off-grid stays planned. The only way to afford the trip was to keep those plans.

I asked around about where I might be able to purchase a propane space heater. Some people told me to go to the Ace Hardware Store. Some people told me to go to the grocery store. Eventually, I drove into the little town and discovered that the Ace Hardware Store was the town grocery store.

The shelf for space heaters was completely empty except for one remaining unit. It was the Mr. Buddy brand. Having spent a lot of time watching all of the Bob Wells videos at CheapRVLiving on YouTube, I knew all about the Mr. Buddy heater. The Mr. Buddy heater is a small propane space heater popular with people who live in repurposed vehicles that don't have furnaces.

Bob Wells sees himself in the service of the poor and the discontented who choose to live as cheaply as possible, often in the cars in which they drove away from their old lives. His lessons are how to survive without any of the conveniences that came built into my Halfloaf. These lessons often mention the Mr. Buddy heater.

One complication was that I wanted to use it on the table so that Happy couldn't get into it. No one on YouTube had ever discussed the use of a Mr. Buddy with a free-roaming bunny. But running it on the table made my ceiling too hot, and I was concerned about damaging my trailer.

I used the Mr. Buddy for one night, protecting my ceiling by turning it on for short periods of time. The next night the furnace started working again, and I've never had another problem with it. Despite having three possible sources of heat (the furnace, the heat strip, and my car), that 25-degree night in the woods remained strong in my memory, and I kept the Mr. Buddy heater for the rest of the year.

RVers who aren't impoverished and who have three kinds of heat might think that the section of the RV world where people like Bob Wells share their tips and tricks has nothing to do with them, but we all live with the same basic needs, and we all need a back-up plan.

The next day I found myself too tired to work, so I decided to get an oil change for the Expedition. Down the street from the RV park was a sort of barn with two car lifts in it. An old man was behind the counter and his young helper was under a lift working on a car. "What's the number for this car?" called out the young man. The older man told him the owner's phone number from memory.

They sent to another town for the oil, and as they didn't take credit cards, I went back to my RV to find enough cash for payment. When I got back, they put my Expedition up on the lift, and I sat on a folding chair in the barn and chatted with the men. A few other people joined us.

When they were done, only half of the car lift would lower. As my car hung sideways on the lift, they bounced it a few times to try to work it free. A local walking by on the sidewalk looked inside and exclaimed, "What the hell!"

He stopped to watch, as did a few more people. Eventually the car was freed, a ribald song I had never heard before was played on a smart phone in celebration, and I was able to leave.

CHAPTER 18

Things That Broke This Year

I HAD BEEN WARNED THAT HAVING AN RV meant dealing with broken things all the time, but in general that hasn't been my experience. When things break, it is expensive for me because of the disability tax (the cost of paying able-bodied people to do things I would otherwise have been able to do myself) and because service contracts don't mean much in the middle of the woods. Fortunately, the things that have broken have been minor and fixable.

When I first got to Miami, a wheel on my Expedition started to sound like a flock of birds squabbling. I took it to a service center associated with my extended warranty provider and found out I had a torn boot on an axle joint. It was all covered under the extended warranty I had purchased, though the service center was very apologetic that it was going to take nearly a week to repair.

This turned out to be a silver lining, as my extended warranty covered a rental car. I had been planning to rent a small car to visit Miami Beach, and now I was saved from the expense and the bother of transporting myself to a rental car company. The service center had a contract for them to come get me. I picked up the car and drove directly to Collins Avenue.

While I was still in Miami, the water heater in my RV went out. In the Miami heat, the water in my tank wasn't exactly cold, so it wasn't that big of an annoyance that it broke. However, the water heater manufacturer turned getting it paid for into one of the biggest annoyances of my trip. People like to complain about the service from the various RV brands, but it's the component makers who are the real jerks.

I had first called a mobile RV tech, thinking it might just be a loose wire. He was horrified at the idea of me without hot water. This very empathetic RV tech came over right away—at a $180 call minimum. RV techs are in short supply. This might be a career to suggest to all the children around you.

He had a little machine to test the hot water controller and within a couple of minutes of arriving at my house had diagnosed a defective controller, a known problem with my water heater. I called the manufacturer and learned that the closest warranty repair center was in the Keys. They would come to my rig, but that would be $400. They wouldn't just ship me a new controller. I was already out $180 to the man I had originally called.

He agreed to come back and install the new controller for a total fee of $200, so just $20 more. And the controller was $250. On any other day, I would have driven to the repair shop. But I had just settled in for two months. Moving my house is enjoyable, but it also comes with stresses like taking care of Happy, especially if I was going to have to park somewhere and wait while my house was repaired. I chose to just pay for the repairs myself.

Then I started to read on the Internet about other people who had been mailed replacement controllers. I got mad. I wrote to the manufacturer expressing my displeasure that I had not been treated like everyone else. It soon became apparent that the reason the manufacturer didn't think we would be comparing notes on social media is they were stuck in the last century.

I got a letter back that they would pay for the replacement controller I had purchased, but only if I sent them an enormous number of documents. I keep all of my personal documents organized electronically, so what may have been an impossible task for someone else was just a couple of clicks for me. I emailed the documents off to the email address on the letter and heard nothing back.

Eventually my mail was forwarded to me, and I found that they had responded to my email with another letter. The letter included a document to sign to receive payment. I signed it and emailed it back.

A while later I got an email that they were sending a man to my domicile the next day, during business hours, to pick up the defective part. Obviously, John wasn't going to take the day off work to meet this man. And the part was with me.

I asked them why they couldn't email me a return shipment tag like every other business in the twenty-first century and was told it simply wasn't something they did. I ended up mailing the defective part to them at my own expense. A total of seven months passed before I received a check, and I was still out more than $200 for this "warranty" coverage.

Aside from the water heater, everything else that went wrong with the trailer was minor enough that I just made a list for repairs at some point in the future. When I returned to North Carolina, I turned in the Halfloaf to the dealer for a week, and they ticked off my list. My door wasn't quite aligned. A light under the bed was installed badly so that there was a wire that I was worried Happy might get at, and the porch light didn't work at all. One arm of my awning got stuck, and somewhere in California the rain cover on my roof vent disappeared. Not a bad list, all things considered and miles covered.

There are horror stories about new RVs all over social media. Some of them are from people who don't have the ability to make the list and get on with life. And some of them are truly horrific cases. I've been fortunate not to have any major issues, but that's not something anyone writes Facebook posts about.

CHAPTER 19

Too Many Friends

AS I WAS HEADING INTO ARIZONA, I CONTACTED Brian, a childhood friend who lived outside Phoenix. At first, we were going to meet at a casino outside Flagstaff, but after my adventure I was too tired to drive there. I suggested he meet me where I was, which was in the middle of nowhere.

"It's close," I said. By which I meant it would have taken me less than a day to drive with the trailer.

"That's not close," Brian said. He was right, of course. And yet he agreed to drive the more than three hours from his house to where I was.

Meanwhile, I discovered that an Internet friend with an Airstream Sport 16 just like mine would be passing through the area as she traveled from one camping area to another. Tara would be there at about the same time as my high school friend who was driving three hours just to see me.

How had I ended up with a social conflict in an Arizona town so remote it was nearly in New Mexico?

Brian arrived with his boyfriend of several years, and we had lunch. We then went back to the Halfloaf and chatted for a while. I was checking my phone like a nervous cat the whole visit, waiting for Tara to arrive.

Even with that effort, I missed her first message and by the time I saw her second message, she only had a few minutes left to stay in town and still make her drive to her next location. So, I threw my friends that had driven three hours to see me out of my house and rushed off to the parking lot where I was meeting Tara.

This was combining the old train math problems with social complications. I've since learned that it is a known risk of living in an RV. I mostly don't tell people where I'm going to be. I don't like train math problems, and I don't have the stamina for social complications. Plus, people think they're going to be able to put me on a schedule—their schedule—when my life doesn't work that way. When I got back to Raleigh, my social calendar ended up getting me confined to my bed for a week.

Staying in RV parks gives some relief from social obligations, but it's not a perfect solution. And I don't want it to be. I am an extremely social person. I've found that it doesn't matter that I have a tiny water tank because if I'm isolated in a forest I will want to get back to people several days before I will run out of water.

Not all RVers have the same social needs as I do. A lot of people who exist somewhere on the spectrum from preferring to be alone to having severe social disabilities love RVing because they can get away from people. Their perspective can make it seem like RVing is a very lonely business, and it can be if you want it to be.

On the other hand, many RVers are extremely outgoing. If I stay in one place long enough to meet my neighbors, I have to put a sign on my door so they don't disturb my naps. It takes something like one day to make good friends, so I have to use the sign pretty much everywhere.

When I slept at the Atchafalaya National Heritage Area Welcome Center, I had met all my neighbors within a couple of hours. The lady parked next to me assured me that her large dog more than made up for the protective deficiencies of my rabbit. This is the kind of community that developed in just one night in a parking lot.

More than once I have stepped outside with my trash and had someone offer to carry it to the trash bin. Once a full-time RVer who wasn't even staying in the same campground as I was offered to loan me his power drill.

Imagine me at my townhouse in Raleigh, going to the next street and asking someone to borrow their drill. This would never happen. When I lived in my house, I could go weeks without speaking to a human being unless I went to Starbucks. RV parks give me a chance to get to know people without getting dressed up and going out, without even walking more than a few feet. When I get too tired, I can turn around and walk right back to my bed. For an extravert with chronic fatigue, it's perfect.

CHAPTER 20

America's National Parks

GETTING FURTHER INTO ARIZONA, I POWERED through the combined Painted Desert National Park and Petrified Forest National Park. One road passes through the two parks. Since I had started from the rural side of things, I came out on the end near I-40. The last time I had been on a freeway was in Austin, TX.

Grand Canyon National Park had originally been on the list of things I wanted to see, but I hadn't realized that you have to drive up to the park from I-40 and then return to I-40 on the same road. Like many people, I loathe backtracking. Also, the visit would take more than a day out of my route, and I was still very tired from my difficult drive across New Mexico.

Because people like to give me to-do lists, someone suggested I take a train or bus up. It astounds me that someone would advise, "You seem tired, what you need in your life is public transportation." This is why we were meant to learn in kindergarten to keep our unsolicited advice to ourselves.

The day Stephen Hawking died brought a flood of images of ableism. The disability community was in a hubbub swatting down thoughtless cartoons and memes. According to the memorial comics, the assistive devices that had given him mobility and the ability to communicate were seen as something to be shed the moment he died. The perfect life, those who shared the images seemed to say, is to be like the able-bodied people who drew them.

What if the perfect life was a world where public transportation is easier than driving? What if we could get on a bus by number instead of having to throw elbows? So often what would make life better for people with disabilities would make life better for everyone. Meanwhile, blotting out someone's mobility device doesn't benefit anyone.

Ultimately, I couldn't bring myself to drive past the turn-off on the freeway. Just off the freeway, I stopped at a turnout for a work conference call. Then I headed up the hill.

When I arrived at the park, the line to get in the

front gate was more than half a mile long. Unknown to me, Paul and Lorena of the YouTube channel The Motorhome Experiment and Laura and Kevin of the channel VeganRV were driving into the park at about the same time as I was. They had been there several times and Paul and Lorena later told me over Facebook that it was an unusually crowded day.

I found an RV parking space near the visitor center. The parking area was a madhouse, with RVs left in the travel lanes and people blocked in by double parkers. The family in the space next to me was blocked in and were still blocked in when I left. Meanwhile, someone had run into the truck that was blocking them in, sending shattered glass across the asphalt.

I made it through the crowd to look over the rim of the canyon, took my pictures, and left. Now I had to decide where to spend the night. Online reviews had indicated that the RV parks were likely sold out. The reviews also said they were overpriced and not very nice anyway. Plus, the hillside was free National Forest land for miles.

I selected a forest road at random and drove past any signs of other people. The first clearing I turned into had a tent at the back. I made an awkward three-point turn and got stuck on the forest leaves that had turned into a slick mat in the clearing. It took four-wheel drive to get off the leaves and back onto the road.

I drove a bit further and found another clearing that was truly unoccupied by people, though marked with the scat of a variety of wild animals. A couple of channels from Flagstaff came through on the television, and I had three bars for Verizon. I was only few miles away from the crowds of the Grand Canyon, but I didn't see another person during my stay. I spent the next two days catching up on my computer until an incoming snowstorm sent me scurrying down the hill.

I really appreciate the YouTube channels of people like The Motorhome Experiment and Vegan RV because they show the places that are difficult for me to go. They spent a long time at the Grand Canyon, walking to many different views and taking pictures. They also have a generator and were confident they could stay through the snowstorm. I don't have to do what they do to think they're awesome.

On the other hand, I cannot count the number of times people have been willing to say aloud, "If you're not going to leave your RV, you might as well not even go to a National Park." First of all, how other people spend their time is none of their business. But it's also a strange duality that says that if my body doesn't work, then the beauty of nature must be of no value to my mind.

This is the mindset that required comics and memes to portray Stephen Hawking as walking through a meadow. The value of a person sitting at the edge of that meadow is discounted. And not just discounted, but discussed with viciousness.

People are afraid to say they have a disability, partly because of this viciousness. People will name their diseases and expect you to intuit what their disabilities might be. Earlier I discussed the self-doubt that comes with chronic fatigue. This doubt follows everyone with a disability. Someone who needs a lot of care, like Stephen Hawking, obviously has a disability, but someone who needs just a little consideration, like someone with chronic fatigue, does not. Unfortunately, this means that people who need a little consideration stay home, even though there is plenty of room for them if only they felt safe articulating their disability and their needs.

No one is going to say that Stephen Hawking's disabilities are his mother's fault because she looked at a rabbit when she was pregnant (an old superstition). But plenty of people are willing to say that someone who is too exhausted to stand in line for a bus tour shouldn't be allowed to enjoy a national park because of whatever their imagined sin is. This is the sort of thing that shames people with disabilities into staying home.

You're too fat, you must never get up from the couch. You're too scrawny, you must never leave the office and go to the gym. No matter what you look like, there's someone out there to tell you your disability is your fault. And not only that, but that you deserve neither care nor consideration, and you certainly don't deserve to enjoy the National Parks.

Please really think about this. Have you ever been in a conversation about just how awful it is that people can see the beauty of Alaska from their cruise ship balcony? Or how wrong it is that people stay in their air conditioned RVs at a National Park? Maybe disrupt these vicious conversations the next time they happen around you.

Later, in California, I found myself driving north on the 101 when I became tired. I saw a sign for Fort Ord National Monument and thought I would take a nap in the parking lot. If there was some kind of fort, there might even be a small museum to see.

It turned out that the National Monument preserves the lands of Fort Ord, and the only development of the property is a small parking lot for hikers. I had come to a park that was literally just for hiking to take my nap. It felt like the perfect middle finger to anyone who thinks disabled people shouldn't use national parks.

CHAPTER 21

Intentional and Unintentional Internet Stalkers

THE RV WORLD IS OBSESSED WITH COUPLES. Back in the entrepreneurial milieu of Research Triangle Park, it was perfectly normal that I and I alone was the president of my company. I interacted with other business people all the time as business people. If they were married or coupled, I may not have even known it.

In contrast, some RVers have a hard time even imagining what it means to be solo. For example, I was at an RV park and I needed to fill my propane. I had asked for propane days earlier and now it was the last day before I was leaving. The man who was supposed to fill my propane, who had not been available for all that time, was going to finish his landscaping work in a few minutes, then a few minutes more, and pretty soon it had been more than hour.

His landscaping was looking dandy and his wife was cooking dinner, but I was standing around waiting to get propane. "Look," I said, " I need you to get this done so I can make dinner," "Oh," he responded, "I didn't realize you were completely out of propane and needed it to make dinner." While I was waiting for him to finish his landscaping, what magical fairy did he imagine was making my dinner? It wasn't about the availability of the propane, it was about the availability of me!

I attended a conference of people who work out of their RVs, and there was so much focus on couple-preneurs (couples who work on a business together) that there was a special session just for solo RVers. I was very eager to be with my people. The session ended up focused on safety, which I found disappointing because that wasn't really the difference I was experiencing.

Anyway, it turned out that the "safety" topic was more of a cover for a metaphysical problem: If I die will anyone notice I am gone? A couple that accidentally drives off a cliff in the wilderness might wonder the same thing, but this was seen as a uniquely solo issue.

It may have been because the solo crowd was younger, and what they were really reflecting was a concern from their parents: If you die will I know that you

are gone? Participants recommended a variety of hor-
rific-sounding electronic leashes they used to keep their
families informed of their location at every moment of
the day and night.

The message is delivered over and over that as a
solo RVer I should be very worried. But when it comes
down to it, the same people are willing to spend zero
energy being worried for me. As an example of just how
carelessly solo RVers are treated, Thousand Trails insists
on printing first names on car and site passes, advertis-
ing where a woman is staying alone. I fold down the
corner where the names start and rip it off every time.
Other people who want to contribute to the safety of solo
RVers can do the same so that the torn pass is not itself
the marker of a solo RVer.

On the Internet, there are RVers who won't talk
to me unless I tell them where I am. Sometimes it is as
lame as someone demanding my location to authenticate
that I am in an RV, even though it has nothing to do with
the topic. You won't give your location, then I win at this
topic. Stupid stuff. Some of it starts out thoughtlessly,
some of it starts out maliciously, but always the demand
is there. This is the only thing that has made me feel
unsafe while RVing.

My advice to anyone managing a social media
site for RVers is to make a rule that you can't ask someone to disclose their location. That one rule would make
social media spaces much more welcoming to solo
women RVers. Let solo women RVers fully participate

without having to edit everything they write to avoid demands for their location.

I quit posting photographs to open Internet sites and groups because there was always someone (in all but one case, a male someone) who wouldn't let it go. I have many beautiful pictures that I would really like to show to people. But I would post some pretty flowers with a range of several states and someone would demand to know the name of the campground. There has not been a single time that I have said I didn't care to share that information and it has been respected. I want to give people the benefit of the doubt that they just aren't thinking, but it never works out that way.

I have seen other people get a response, "Sorry, I didn't think through what I was asking." That has never happened to me. When I suggest people do think about what they're asking, for me to share my location with the entire Internet, they have invariably become argumentative and abusive.

One time an Airstream Pan American pulled in next to me. This is an extremely rare Airstream, and in my excitement, I posted a photograph to an Airstream-related social media group immediately. A man asked to know where I was. I answered that I had posted what I was comfortable posting. He persisted in demanding to know where I was.

For some reason I just deleted the picture instead of deleting him. He went and found an older post of mine and began harassing me there! So then I had to delete that post as well, and of course I blocked him. The reason I had to delete the post was that if I left it up other people would join the conversation to advise me what I should have done differently not to be harassed. Only once has someone pointed out that the man should stop harassing me.

Before I blocked him, the end of our conversation revealed something. He felt that I should post my location because he was telling me he wasn't a threat. Never mind that what he was demanding was that I post my location for the entire Internet to read. "I'm not that interested in you," he wrote. That's not better, it's worse: he was willing to casually endanger me for no particular reason.

In his case, for some reason he was certain he would be able to see this RV if he knew where it was. Of course, that's ludicrous. First, it could have been anywhere in the country. But more importantly, it was a unique and special experience. I had happened to be staying at the same RV park and had happened upon the owner when he was outside and not pressed for time. You don't get that just by showing up in the same place.

Nonetheless, some have a grim determination that the only way to have the experience seen on the Internet is to go to the exact same place someone else has gone. That's not how it works. Even if you go to the same place, how you got there would be different. You wouldn't have seen it on a map and decided to give it a try. You wouldn't have had the same experiences in the

week before, and the same weather, and the same neighbors, and all the things that make each experience unique.
Recreating the geography of someone else's experience
doesn't recreate the reality of it.

Many of us know that from the trajectory of our
own lives. How often have you returned to a magical
place only to find it wasn't as magical as you remembered? Magical experiences exist within the currents of
our lives and flow into the past on those same currents.
If there is anything to be learned from this book, it is not
the coordinates of a specific campsite where I stayed, but
rather the tools available to find your own way.

CHAPTER 22

An Outdoorswoman Who Doesn't Go Outdoors

LEAVING THE GRAND CANYON, I DROVE WEST on I-40 through light snow. Outside Kingman, Arizona, I turned off the freeway at a truck stop and headed up the hill. Freecampsites.net had shown camping spaces available on BLM (Bureau of Land Management, federal land) property up the road. The cement ended and the dirt road continued up the hill, away from the sound of the freeway. Eventually there was a sign stating that I had crossed onto BLM property and asking me to leave my name in a sign-in log.

Up the hill a bit more I turned onto a dirt road, and then another that cut through the heavy brush just wide enough for my trailer. Eventually, I found a clearing next to the road that had been created when the bulldozer that cleared the road had dumped some excess dirt into the bushes. Going back over the road, he had left a berm that my trailer would have a little bit of trouble getting over.

What I had to do was dip into the clearing with my car, allowing the trailer to get one wheel up onto the berm. Now with the sewer connection, bumper, and other vital bits lifted a bit, I could back the other tire up over the berm and then straighten out to get backed into the clearing.

Pulling forward to change my angle, I didn't look in front of me. I was in the middle of nowhere. In fact, I was several dirt roads away from nowhere. Still, some small movement or sound caused me to jerk my head around to check out the front of my truck.

I found myself facing a big, flat expanse of metal that was the side of a FedEx truck, seemingly inches from my nose. I was intensely embarrassed to have pulled forward without looking. Every responsible driver looks where they are driving, even when they haven't seen a single sign of civilization for miles, don't they? I could barely meet the eyes of the driver. He gave a little wave and continued on. I never saw the FedEx truck come back, and in the three days I stayed up there that was the only person or vehicle I saw.

Staying in a place like this is called boondocking,

a play on the word "boondocks," as you are far away from urban areas. Sometimes it is also called "dry camping," which is a thing you can do in an urban area as well as on a mountain side.

Some people's boondocking sites end up looking like small military installations. Mom and Dad may take this opportunity to put each kid in a tent and have the RV to themselves. Sometimes dogs and cats even get their own tents. Twice I've seen people set up entire offices in screen tents, complete with three large monitors wrapping around a workstation. Once I saw someone set up an entire baking station in a tent and make a cake that looked like it came from a fancy shop.

My boondocking spots, in contrast, look abandoned. My illness forces me to be efficient. I never bought a grill, because I knew I didn't have the energy to maintain one. I did buy an outdoor rug and an outdoor table and folding chair so I could sometimes work outside.

Of course, all of that stuff is long gone, another lesson in the errors of "pre-need" purchases. I occasionally use a medication that makes me sensitive to sunlight, and anyway I don't have the energy to put that stuff up and take it back down. I work at a chair right by my front door. If I open the door, I'm as good as outside. My bed is very comfortable for lounging and is situated directly against a large window. I have everything I need already set up.

Earlier, in Texas, I had stayed a few days at a free

municipal RV park. The stop afforded an opportunity to observe some of the antics of the able-bodied. Among the players was a family that pulled in next to me in a huge fifth wheel. The RV park was parking lot-style, and out onto the asphalt came an entire living room, with furnishings including a huge outdoor rug, lounging furniture, a table and chairs. When they were done setting up, they unfolded a walker and brought an elderly woman out from the truck.

The elderly woman went into the trailer for a while and then was brought back out and sat at the table while the man of the family grilled some food and the younger woman, perhaps his wife, set the table. I don't think anyone could fault me for thinking these folks were going to be my new neighbors for a day or two. But after lunch, they packed everything up and left. I am surprised when people unfold a sewer tube support to stay somewhere one night, but this was a whole different level.

The set-up for lunch was remarkably civilized. If someone wants to spend their time that way, that's fine. But there are so many other things, like using a sewer tube support for one day, that are just wasted energy. I do sometimes think the able-bodied RVer might learn a thing or two from someone who has to be more efficient.

CHAPTER 23

Finding My Food

I WAS STANDING IN LINE AT AN RV EVENT when the couple in front of me was delivered special plates. Choosing not to eat what the rest of us were eating, they had plates heaped high with kale and other vegetables that I can't eat due to my illness.

They had done nothing wrong and were just eating their own food, but the specter of orthorexia hangs over every American encounter with food. Other people started to comment about the superiority of their food choices. There is nothing good about commenting on other people's food. You shouldn't comment on other people's food.

"I can't eat any of that," I said, commenting on their food. They were curious and I explained a little about my illness. They were more than polite, they were good and kind and interested. I have never seen them to be anything else. But the conversation left me unsettled.

Eating is one of the spark points where inaccurate ideas about health and the healthy converge into one hot mess. If healthy people can eat kale, for example, then clearly eating kale is healthy. The idea that the behavior of healthy people creates health becomes a self-referential fetish. The idea that these same behaviors might make other people sick is something of a head scratcher.

And yet one of the main drivers of my food choices is a genetic factor that is about 50/50 in people of Eastern European heritage. It shouldn't be a secret that different people need different food to be healthy and that orthorexia makes about as much sense as thinking that since insulin is life-saving for a diabetic person, it should be injected into everyone.

Even more than when living in a house, living in an RV requires a multi-point juggling game of finding the food that is right for you. No one is eating the same thing. Each individual has their taste preferences, every body has its nutritional preferences, and local community purchasing power and decisions shape what is actually available at the grocery store. When you're living in an RV, reaching a town with a major grocery store can be heavenly, and food shipping services like Amazon can be a lifesaver.

RVs also have issues with limited space, and everyone has to take what they can afford into their decision matrix. Food is my fourth-largest expense after health insurance, student loans, RV parks, and gas.

My refrigerator has three shelves (counting the bottom as a shelf) and a small freezer. It cools very unevenly, with the top right freezing and the bottom left about room temperature. I usually stuff whatever meat I have in the top right and put things I'm less concerned about on the bottom. The bottom usually has two cartons of eggs and some cheese.

Happy's box of salad greens takes up half of the middle shelf. The other side is stuffed with whatever is left, generally containers of sauces and dressings and maybe a soda. Butter, water, and a small container of milk for my morning tea are in the door.

I have one cabinet filled with teas over my kitchen counter. Just like when I lived in a house, I mainly drink the same ones and the rest will be thrown out after a year or two when they've lost any hope of flavor. I have one box of dry goods. Bob Wells recommends having a large bag of rice so that wherever you are, you can get across the country in an emergency without needing to buy food. My bag is in a storage container in the back of my car.

Having a complex illness adds yet another dimension to the issue. Many people with complex illnesses report becoming fearful about food. We develop our own personal orthorexia matrix. Over the years various foods have been implicated in my illness, then redeemed, then tried and found guilty again. After a while, so many foods were on the chopping block that there was almost nothing left to eat, and I found myself eating whatever was making me the least sick that week.

I started eating ingredients more than meals. When you are sick, meals can be terrifying because you are never certain what has happened to you. As I was traveling, I had a potentially deadly health event that could have been caused by a food I had eaten. My doctor reviewed each ingredient over the phone. I had made my dinner from scratch and only used six ingredients. Which one was it? I didn't eat any of them again for more than three months.

I wasn't completely realistic about how I would prepare my food when I moved into my RV. I threw out a blender in my house that I hadn't used in years, but I bought a stick blender set up that takes half of a kitchen cabinet that I also haven't used.

The Halfloaf doesn't have an oven, so before I moved in, I purchased an Instant Pot and learned how to use it. The Instant Pot has been an excellent addition, and I have cooked everything from cinnamon rolls to steaks in it.

I need to go grocery shopping about once a week. Running out of food is my number one problem with food. It's not just the small amount of space in the Halfloaf, it's my behavior around food that can be like a small child. If I'm going to go park on public land for a while, you know what happens: I eat all the good stuff on the first day, and I'm ready to wrestle my rabbit for his salad by the last day.

At that point, I drag myself back to town. If it's cool, I can drive straight to the grocery store. If it's hot, I have to unhitch so Happy can stay at an RV park with air conditioning. Consequently, grocery shopping can be a two-day project: first unhitching, and then grocery shopping the next day.

If I'm feeling well, I am likely to go out to a restaurant once a week or so. It is, after all, a pleasure one can enjoy sitting down. Also, my cooking tends to be repetitive, and I tell myself the nutritional variety is good for me.

I don't carry a grill. I don't have the space to store it, and I don't have the energy to set it up and maintain it. Yet my body requires a high animal protein diet. So every week to 10 days, I go somewhere and eat a giant steak, and it restores me.

As my first year in my RV was passing, it seemed like not a single restaurant had a steak that tasted any good. Mass market foods were getting lower and lower in quality, I complained. I went to a brunch restaurant with a friend and the food tasted like it had been made for a movie set. I threw a small fit about the fake foods restaurants were serving these days. I bought cilantro in the middle of the country and it tasted like parsley. I came up with a theory about how long shipping was destroying food.

At the end of the year, I ended up changing my medication and suddenly everything tasted good again. It turned out I had lost my sense of taste. My irrational responses to the condition weren't unusual. In medical studies, asking people if they have lost their sense of taste gets extremely inaccurate answers. (Testing is the only way to find out.) I apologize to all the restaurants I accused of serving fake food.

CHAPTER 24

A Long Run to Safety

ON MY DRIVE TO CALIFORNIA, I HAD MOSTLY been boondocking, but once I passed the agricultural inspection station at the California state line, it was clear things had changed. Even though the landscape was still a wilderness, fences stretched along both sides of the freeway as far as the eye could see. All of California is one big "no parking" sign.

Eventually I found a place to pull over and look up where I might want to stop for the night. My best choices were a Historic Route 66 diner that let anyone stay for a night and also was listed as a Harvest Hosts member or the Calico Ghost Town. At the ghost town, I would have to pay, but I would have electricity if I needed to run my air conditioner and free admission into a ghost town that included a Starbucks.

I picked the ghost town and arrived during an enormous Boy Scout event. The space I was assigned had tents pressed up against each side surrounding the space, and boys running everywhere. I backed in without sacrificing a Boy Scout and went to sleep with my air conditioner on. When I got up in the morning, they were all gone, and I was completely alone in the canyon.

Cautious of ghosts, I picked my way around the canyon until I found the stairs up to the town. The ghosts had the last laugh because though I found a Starbucks, they didn't carry decaf. Several different aspects of my illness make consuming the amount of caffeine in coffee a bad idea. No Starbucks for me.

I looked through the little shops and in the back of one, I found white supremacist items—t-shirts and key rings and such. These things are usually just under the surface but sometimes are in your face. I've seen more white supremacist RV flags than I can recount. Later, when I acquired my own personal white supremacist in an iffy situation in Kansas, I would be conflicted about taking advantage of the situation.

I had lunch and returned to my rig to read some study materials. California is known for going after taxation of income generated in the state, so it's best to just find something else to do. I also looked up where I was going to go next.

Full-time RVers tend to spend a lot of time in the desert. It's free and, unlike most federal land, you can get permits to stay for longer than two weeks in some places. For many people, the desert is an affordable stop in the winter instead of the mortgage-level prices of RV parks in Florida. I've thought about trying a long-term stay in the dessert, but it's a bit too far north of where I know works for my health. And I have to admit that I don't really enjoy the desert.

In fact, by this time, all I wanted was to be out of the desert. Kingman had been on the edge, but this was just too desolate for my soul. I looked at routes to get to the Central Coast where I would be visiting my dad. I decided to head to Santa Clarita next. Google Maps wanted to route me through L.A. to get to the ranch. Going to Santa Clarita forced a northern route that stayed out of the most congested areas of Southern California.

As I got back into civilization, I found a real Starbucks, but I had to park far down the street. After I parked, the area struck me as a bit too shady, and I decided not to leave my car there. Really, I could handle losing my belongings, and I always carry with me the computer that is essential to my work. But I wouldn't be able to stand it if anything happened to Happy, so that makes me a lot more cautious about where I leave my rig.

Eventually, I found another Starbucks and glee-fully purchased some tangible proof that I was back in the real world. What an odd thing that I had passed by a ghost town Starbucks on the way there.

Unfortunately, the real world involved road construction. As I pulled out of the parking lot, I discovered the hard way that the drop off from the sidewalk to the road that had been dug out for resurfacing was extra deep. I dragged the bumper of the Airstream on the edge of the sidewalk, pushing it up and damaging every single piece of it.

The Sport 16 is Airstream's budget model, and as such, it doesn't come with a bumper. I had paid almost $2,000 to have the bumper added so that it might protect the trailer if I were to back into a tree. Now I was in a situation where I had done $2,000 worth of damage when there would have been no damage at all if I didn't have the bumper.

Worse, the higher-end parks I was headed toward don't allow damaged RVs. If they didn't let me in, "no parking" California was going to give me a run for my money. I had no way of knowing a run for my money was exactly where I was headed.

I had looked up two RV parks in Santa Clarita. One park was managed by the local government, but the reviews mentioned that shady people stayed there. A very nice KOA was a few feet away. I drove over to the government park and paid the rate to drive in and look around. I had selected a spot and decided to stay there when a few things delayed my ability to go back and pay for the space. As I was waiting, I got more uneasy about the place and decided the delay was a sign I should leave.

I drove over to the KOA and found that it was gone. Though it was still listed on the KOA website and the Allstays app for finding RV parks, it had been destroyed by the fire that had come through the area the previous summer. I sent in a report to Allstays. Adam, the owner of the app, made an experiment of checking out just how far the KOA website would let him go booking a stay at the burned-out park.

When I drove back by the government park, the sheriff was there. I thought it meant I had made a good decision to leave. I was right, I just didn't know the reason, and I didn't know the reason was going to chase me deep into the night. Meanwhile, I continued toward the coast.

I don't usually make reservations before I see an RV park with my own two eyes, but there were very few choices left to me, and I was going to be tired by the time I got to the coast, so I called ahead and made a reservation.

When I got to the coast, I checked in, but before I even got to my site, a man in a golf cart drove up beside me and handed me a packet of evacuation information. I was to be ready to evacuate within an hour of notice. Heavy rain was coming in and landslides were expected on the hillsides recently scarred by fire. The sheriff back in Santa Clarita had probably been evacuating the campground.

I checked my maps and saw that there was

nowhere to stay between the edge of the danger zone and the central coast. If I decided to leave now, my only choice was going to be to drive for several more hours, and I was already exhausted. I had already driven twice as far as I normally do in a day.

Also, I was ticked that they had taken my money and only then given me the evacuation information. They knew they were in an evacuation zone when I called, and they hadn't told me. It took a complaint to the California Attorney General and challenging the credit card payment before they would give me my money back. It's the only time I've ever demanded my money back from a campground. They certainly had no right to keep it.

If I decided to stay, I was going to have to unhitch to fit into my site. I could then end up having to hitch up to evacuate in the middle of the night on crowded roads with nowhere to go. I try not to hitch up and do any other physical activity on the same day to reduce the chance of having a chronic fatigue crash. I was already tired from the long drive.

That was the best-case scenario. The worst-case scenarios were that my home was destroyed or that Happy or I died. The only reasonable choice was to leave immediately.

For the second time that day, I left a camp site and continued on in search of my fourth campground. I had a two-week reservation in Pismo Beach, near my father's ranch, starting two days later. I turned north on the 101. If I couldn't get into a campground in Pismo Beach, I could stay at Dad's place.

Up until this point, I had been somewhat blasé about knowing exactly where I was. Actually, I still am, though I've had several opportunities to learn my lesson. I had already been sent to a shelter by audible sirens when a tornado passed two miles from my campsite. Of course, I had no way to know it was that close because I had no idea where I was.

Another time, in Texas, an alarm had gone off, and I had no idea what danger it might represent or where I was meant to go. I never went anywhere and I survived, so perhaps it was just a test alarm. But now I had driven straight into a known high-risk area.

What I did right was keep some space in my time and energy, some "extra spoons." My original plan didn't stretch me to the limits of my capabilities, so as the plan changed again and again, requiring more and more out of me, I was able to keep going.

I was both lucky and prepared. This kind of over-exertion could have set me back for a month. On the other hand, I always plan to get to my campsite by the mid-afternoon so that if something does go wrong, I have some energy left to try another option. Though I was tired by the time it was all over, I was well within bounds to recover after a good sleep or two. And it just so happened that this time, I recovered very well by the next day.

CHAPTER 25

My Childhood Home

THE NEXT DAY, DAD CAME TO GET ME AND took me out to lunch. Since I was going to my originally intended Thousand Trails destination the next day, I didn't unhitch.

While he was there, he looked at my bumper and the closet where I wanted shelves installed. The shelves were a "Dad project," something that would be hard to find someone else to do, so that was my priority. Plus, Dad had already grumbled a little about assumptions on his labor. I called a trailer shop to work on the bumper.

After feeling extremely capable while living in

my RV and driving across the country, being in my home-town of Arroyo Grande pulled me up short. I hadn't felt disabled, but now that I was back in a place where what I had been able to do last time I visited was in sharp con-trast to what I was able to do this time, I did.

The last time I had visited, I had gone to the famed San Luis Obispo Farmers Market. Even then I hadn't been able to do much, but by arriving early I was able to slip into the line for some McClintock's ribs. I then went back to my car and drove back to the time-share where I was staying to eat them. I had walked to a restaurant every day for lunch, but even then, I had to count my spoons and got nervous about getting too tired.

As a child, I had wanted nothing more than to drive forever and never come home. A male teacher, familiar with all the complications of my life, tried to extol Thelma and Louise as heroes. "But they're dead," I said. "On their own terms," he replied. "Still dead!" I said.

Stuck in my first marriage, I watched as Susan Smith couldn't even dream of driving away and drove into a lake. Years later I read in *Travels with Charlie* where Steinbeck wrote that he too had not been able to drive away from his life, admitting he only maintained the illusion for the sake of the reader.

At one point, I got a job where my actual job was to fly away from everything in my life. The job involved flying all around the country to inspect documents at medical centers and hospitals. The very beginning of my career was before companies gave their road warriors cell phones, and it was years before cell phones would be routinely used for data connections. The job required leaving everything behind, and I loved it.

But now I had other tasks that I had to complete at my desk. My dad came by with Meghan and Erik, relatives of his wife, Betsy, (my mother died years ago) and took the bumper off my trailer. Dad had come around to deciding to fix it and wanted to try to straighten it out some in his shop before I brought the trailer over to put it back on and get my closet shelves installed.

The next day, I brought the trailer out to the ranch so Dad and Erik could work on it. My old superpower of tenacity is only a tiny percentage of what my dad has. My dad can work from sunup to sundown, even now in his mid-seventies. When I was a child, Dad would get frustrated when I needed a break from weeding a field after three hours. I was a little worried about how he would respond to my disability now that we had a project.

Fortunately, Dad and Erik had gelled after several days of ranch work, so I didn't have to be part of the project. I stood around trying to look appropriately engaged, appreciative, and grateful (and keeping an eye on how careful they were with Happy, who was asleep under my dinette). When that became too exhausting, I took a nap. Later, I drove to town and had lunch with one of my high school teachers.

When I came back, they were still working on the shelves. I had rejected some ratty wood pulled from

the back of the barn, and they had gone to town and purchased just enough wood to finish the project. A small
mistake sent them all the way back to town for more
wood. Before they had even started on the shelves, they
had fixed and re-attached the bumper.

Nothing in an Airstream is a straight line, so
every shelf had to be cut for its individual place. And the
whole thing had to fit around the water heater access and
an electrical box in the closet. The sun started to set, and
Erik tried to tap out. "We could finish this tomorrow,"
he said. They had been working for 10 hours without
a break. I was so glad to get to watch this one play out.
"There's probably just another hour of work," Dad said.
He was neither grim nor gleeful nor even tired. He was
entirely focused on the work, and what the work wanted
was one more hour. That's my dad.

They worked another hour, and I started packing
up before he could think of any more work that needed to
be done. I reached around Dad's feet and grabbed Happy
and put him in the back of the car. Ten minutes later Dad
suddenly asked, sounding a little stressed, where the
rabbit was. I regretted making him worry, but I was also
glad to hear he was worried about my dear pet.

Finally, they were done, and I was able to drive
back to the campground. I had to be back at Dad's the
next day for Easter lunch, so I had to unhitch that night
after a very long day.

The next morning, I grabbed a Starbucks and
headed back to the ranch. For years, Betsy has provided

an enriching environment for a woman with profound developmental disabilities. She had been sprung from her group home for the holiday, and the first project was setting up an Easter egg hunt for her. We then ate lunch off a beautifully set table.

After lunch, everyone decided to walk back to a pond on the ranch. It was much further than I could possibly walk, so I sat down on the couch, intending to entertain myself until their return. I was really touched that Dad offered to get his ATV and take me on a ride around the ranch instead. I hadn't been sure how he would react to my disability, and this was very special.

I had a few tears leaving Arroyo Grande on the 101. I used to worry about whether my parents would be alive when I came back, but now I worry more about whether I'll be healthy enough to come back or what sort of experience I will have if I do. The touchstone of this slowly changing place puts my increasing disability in front of my face. It is way too clear what I have lost.

I drove into the seaside town of Morro Bay and out onto the parking area near Morro Rock. I took a short walk on the seashore and then spent the rest of the afternoon in the Halfloaf. Out there by the ocean, I napped and made my lunch. Years before I would have been out in the water in the speed and drama of a sailboat race. Now I was able to enjoy the same space but from the gentle cocoon of my RV.

CHAPTER 26

Driveway Surfing

THAT NIGHT I STAYED IN THE DRIVEWAY OF Max and Helen Sicher, parents of one of my childhood friends. I hadn't known that they had been spending part of their winters in Quartzsite, Arizona, in an old Class A. Quartzsite is famous among full-time RVers as a winter hangout, one of the few places in America where you can stay on federal land for longer than 14 days. Hardly anyone else knows that the town—year-round population 3,677—exists, so I was delighted at the unexpected connection.

For breakfast, they took me to the Coffee Pot

Restaurant in Morro Bay. The owner, Lu Chi Fa, had come to town just as I was leaving 20 years earlier. Mr. Lu had an amazingly warm spirit. He hugged me and gave me a mug with the restaurant logo. I didn't even know his story at that point nor how famous his spirit had become.

Mr. Lu is the author of *Double Luck: Memoirs of a Chinese Orphan*, the story of his unlikely path from a childhood that repeatedly cycled loss, disappointment, and abuse to achieving his lifelong dream of owning a restaurant in the United States. But more importantly, the book described how he maintained his very special spirit through all of those experiences. I live in 100 square feet, so I gave away the mug and the book that I purchased and read, but the story remains in my heart.

My next stop was in Santa Cruz at the home of a couple who had advertised on Boondocker's Welcome. This is a website where people advertise to let you stay in their driveway for free. They have a very small reward: a free membership on Boondocker's Welcome for their own stays. The main reward seems to be the entertainment value of visits from travelers and their stories.

The couple was delightful and kind. I scraped their driveway very badly with the bottom of my hitch coming in, but they didn't seem to mind. The husband even got on his hands and knees beside my trailer and put down some boards to make sure my sewer connection made it over the curb. I felt some pressure to be entertaining enough to be worth the trouble!

Normally, I wouldn't unhook for just two nights, but their driveway didn't have enough room and I didn't have a choice. Once free, I drove a couple of blocks away for dinner. The next day I walked around the block admiring the gardens and flowers in the beautiful neighborhood. Relatives that live in the area came and got me and took me to a seafood restaurant overlooking a harbor.

I've never had a visit to Santa Cruz that was anything less than magical, and this visit did not disappoint. The atmosphere of the ocean and the trees doesn't allow for anything other than joy. To be able to stay right in town in my own bed was delightful.

The final driveway of this little streak of driveway surfing was in Palo Alto. Driveway surfing is also called "moochdocking." After all of my stays in woods and deserts, I was amazed to also have my house in the heart of urban comforts. I ordered food delivery right to my front door and took a rideshare to Starbucks.

I also spent two weeks at the Encore RV park directly overlooking the ocean in Pacifica, but these driveways were the best parts of my time in California.

CHAPTER 27

One Afternoon in Tahoe

LEAVING THE BAY AREA, I STOPPED TO VISIT relatives and then spent the night at the base of the Sierra Nevada mountains at a Harvest Host farm stand. The next morning, I drove up the mountain toward Tahoe, intending to stay at a Sno-Park location. Sno-Park is a program among a few states where parking lots are provided and kept clear of snow. All Sno-Park locations are available for daily parking and a few are available for overnight parking.

After driving into the wooded mountains and stopping along rushing rivers, I reached the first location

I had selected. It was a bit outside Tahoe, and I still needed to stop somewhere and purchase my Sno-Park passes. As with many places where daily passes also allow overnight parking, I would need two passes to park for one night.

Soon after I left the Sno-Park, I reached the grade down into Tahoe. It was the most terrifying thing I have driven—anywhere. I went down it in first gear, and I still needed to use my brakes. I would bring my rig to an almost complete stop, and then let go of the brake. As the rig accelerated toward 20 miles per hour, I would repeat the process.

By the time I got down the grade, there was no way I was going to return to that Sno-Park since it would mean driving down that grade again. I stopped at a gas station, purchased my Sno-Park passes, and continued on to the next parking lot.

The next parking lot was across the road and out of view of the lake but had a good view of a mountain. It was next to what seemed to be a public road, but gated, going into a neighborhood. At the very back of the parking lot was one elderly rig. I took a spot near the front.

I took a nap and then looked around the Internet a bit. I was particularly interested in finding out more about the Sno-Park program. What I discovered was that the website listing was the primary rule for whether a lot was open for overnight parking. There may not be a "no overnight parking" sign, but if the website said no overnight parking, that was it. And where I was parked was marked on the website as no overnight parking.

I found another Sno-Park on the map and continued on counter-clockwise around the lake. The road was amazing, soaring up into the mountains and then plunging back into ravines. Almost every turn had a view of Tahoe Lake. I wouldn't have wanted to drive it in anything larger than my rig, but at 16 feet I could easy manage the narrow twisting road.

Arriving at my third Sno-Park, I found laminated signs that explained that just for that one night no overnight parking was allowed. It appeared that they intended to resurface the lot in the morning.

A couple of small Class C rigs were tucked into the forest next to the lot, but the trees were too close together for me to find the 35 feet of open space that I would need. Plus, I'm too much of a rule follower to spend the night next to the road. Parking on national forest land is legal in most places, but the rules vary from forest to forest. Generally, you have to be at least a quarter mile from a paved road or developed site. I was tired, but it was still early enough that I could make it to the casino parking lot in Carson City if I kept moving.

The closest rig to the road was old and painted a stealthy matte black. I had three Sno-Park passes that there was no way I could use, but perhaps this guy could. I walked over to where the person would be able to see me out the window, but still a respectful distance away from the rig, and explained to the rig that I was leaving the area and would like to give him my Sno-Park Passes.

You don't need to knock on the door of an RV. We have windows and thin walls. When you knock on the door, especially in my tiny trailer, you are knocking right in my face. You might as well be inside my house. If I only have the screen door closed, you are literally inside my house, basically inside my bedroom.

It's very intrusive and there is no need for it. What if I'm on the toilet or napping? Do I have to come to the door just because you knocked? What if I'm sitting here at my chair by the door working? Why are you in my house when I am working? And if I don't know you, I'm not opening the door unless I know what you want, especially in the woods.

I could hear someone bounding through the rig, and a thin black man with dreads tied up into a crown flew out the door. This was the moment I felt like a real RVer. I had known all the correct etiquette for how to deal with another RVer and behaved myself properly, and a total stranger in the woods had decided I was worth talking to.

I explained that the lot had the signs up and that I was done trying to find a Sno-Park and was headed to Carson City and wanted to give him my passes. He took them with thanks and told me I should park in the woods with him. "The police come and try to bust my balls," he said, "But I'm on National Forest land so I just tell them to go away."

I wasn't going to debate that even if he wasn't under their jurisdiction, he still wasn't legal, so I just pointed out that there wasn't any room for me to pull in. I was a bit amazed that a black man would stand up to the police in the woods when he was totally in the wrong. And that it worked.

He handed the passes back to me. "You should just park on that lot. They aren't going to work on it until tomorrow. No one is going to tell you to leave." I hesitated. The lot was elevated over the road, and I would have a beautiful view of the lake from my trailer. And I was tired and didn't really want to drive to Carson City.

But I also didn't want any trouble, and if they kicked me out when I was even more tired, I would really be in a pickle. None of the RV parks around Tahoe had opened yet, and my only choice would be to drive down the mountain in the dark. I handed the passes back to him.

He started to compliment the Halfloaf and wanted to have a conversation, but I was so tired and my goal was to make sure I was done driving before I was really miserable. I wish I had taken the time. Maybe I should have even taken the risk of spending the night in that parking lot so we could have had a real conversation. I would like to have known his story.

CHAPTER 28

Am I Homeless?

A FEW MONTHS LATER I PULLED INTO A campground on the edge of Verizon coverage and asked if I could check the Internet speed at my spot before I paid. A boomer in a plaid shirt and khakis behind me sneered, "You're camping!"

Calmly I said, "I'm full-time, and I have a job."

"Good for you," retorted the wife.

"Homelessness" is at its core about being demeaned. If I'm not homeless, there are days when I'm sure doing that wrong.

"But you have a choice," is the reply. This reply

both overemphasizes my own options and underemphasizes the options of people who are truly homeless, presumably, people without choice. The majority of homeless children are those with diverse sexual identities who have been rejected by their families. They had a choice to "look straight." Who would demand they make that choice? Or even call it a choice?

There's an old story about a rich man who goes to an after party and meets the maestro violinist who just played at Carnegie Hall. "Sir, I would give anything to play Carnegie Hall," the man says. "I have," responds the violinist. Excluding some aspect of talent, which is always worth far less than focus, each of these people had a choice to become who they are. Yet we know that they wouldn't be anyone else. Their places actually can't be exchanged.

Certain existentialists use the term "commitment" to mean committing to this reality. Unlike popular misconceptions about existentialism, it isn't a teaching that reality is anything you want it to be. Rather, it is the radical commitment that allows reality to become the servant of your choice.

If I were to say that I was forced to give up everything I owned and become homeless, it is true. But it is also not true. I had so many other options. I could have stayed in my house and maybe I would have found a way to make that work. I could have moved into an apartment. I could have struggled until I could document a lack of choice and become legally disabled.

I could have lost and while I was losing gained nothing. Is that a choice? If it is, I took the easy way out—lose everything and win living in an RV as my prize. I won dignity and self-respect. Rude though that couple was, they couldn't take any of that away from me.

And I'm winning in how I express my dignity—however rude that man was, my reader is inclined to see things from my point of view, because I'm close enough to the range of middle-class life, broadly understood, that you can relate to me. Would you have taken my side if that same man had kicked me off the sidewalk in front of his business?

I was at a business dinner in the fall when the topic of homelessness came up. No one knew a homeless person was at the table and as their conversation continued, I was less and less inclined to speak up. I corrected them with a few statistics, but the conversation centered entirely upon people who are homeless as a nuisance. The problem was not that different from bird droppings on the sidewalk. You powerwash it away, and it disappears from existence.

That the people would not disappear so easily without changes to policy didn't seem to enter their minds. In the particular geographic area under discussion, 50 percent of homeless people were employed. They didn't need law enforcement or healthcare; they needed homes. What about the public policy that makes those homes unavailable? Many areas are thousands of units of housing behind due to regulatory failures and failures to respond to housing needs that were forecast decades ago.

Full-time RVers talk a lot about what it means to be homeless. How do you define homelessness so that we're not homeless? Often, they focus on choice, because choice is the way that we experience our own dignity. But not being "homeless" isn't about choice, it's about the dignity others are willing to afford us.

Being around RV people means being around a lot of people who are broken in some way or at least would appear to be to the world they have removed themselves from. RV parks are where those who have been powerwashed from humanity show up. Perhaps this is why RV people are usually so nice to each other. Everyone knows what it is to need help. Not only that, but they've found a way to live where and how their life doesn't break them. They're not so quick to break other people.

RV parks are by no means racially integrated. This is something that many RVers come to find disappointing. But they are probably the most economically integrated communities in America. A half-million-dollar Class A motor coach can be parked next to a thousand-dollar trailer owned by someone struggling to stay housed on minimum wage.

This can be a very comfortable space for a disabled person who is neither here nor there. I find myself with one foot in the upper middle class and one foot hanging on to the bottom rung of the American economic ladder. On any given day, my life can be either experience—or sometimes both.

Before I left my previous life, I belonged to an exclusive club for business people. The terror of disability and the possibility of poverty was something that could never be mentioned. In the RV park, it's something that doesn't have to be mentioned. The RV park is often that safe space everyone is looking for, where you don't have to explain yourself.

CHAPTER 29

An Unhappy Bunny
in Carson City

I THOUGHT I WAS ONLY GOING TO SPEND A
night or two at the casino in Carson City, but when I got
there, Happy refused to eat his hay or pellets. Usually
when he is off his food, he'll still eat lettuce. This time
he deteriorated until he would only eat the lettuce if I fed
it to him one leaf at a time.

A rabbit is essentially a support system for a bacterial colony. The rabbit lives off of the byproducts of the
bacteria. If the rabbit stops eating, the bacterial colony
collapses. If the bacterial colony collapses, the rabbit dies.

I carry a rabbit pharmacy with me, including a special feeding solution that can be mixed with water and then pushed into his throat with a feeding syringe. I started feeding him with it and looked up the closest rabbit vet in case we needed more help. Sometimes IV fluids can help keep a bunny going until he is ready to eat.

Veterinarians we have seen have encouraged me to start using the feeding solution earlier, but that has never seemed the right approach with this rabbit. I feel it's not so much about the food, but about encouraging Happy to find the will to live. I pet him, I give him stomach and intestine massages and I set him in front of his food and water dishes every few hours. Even if I feed him solution, at some point he has to decide to eat for himself.

When I was ready to sell my house, I had three pet rabbits. Two were rebound bunnies, purchased after the early death of a sweet and cuddly Angora named Brewster. Over the course of 10 years waiting for them to die so I could get rabbits I actually liked, they came to be known as the Substandard Replacement Bunnies. Those bunnies went to a family with a young girl who loved them and, surprising everyone, they loved her back.

The remaining rabbit, Happy, I had taken from the rabbit rescue only on the understanding that I could see if we actually liked each other and take him back if we didn't. I didn't want to make a mistake with another rabbit. Happy turned out to be funny and opinionated and cuddly. He romped on my bed at three a.m. and made adorable squeaking protests when he was caught doing something naughty.

Pets have always served an important emotional role for me, and I couldn't see living without one. And Happy, in particular, I couldn't give up. He is elderly, mostly deaf and mostly blind. He turns his head slowly from side to side in a behavior called "scanning," trying to put together a visual reference of what is going on around him.

Rabbits are fragile creatures to start with, and I wasn't sure how Happy would do traveling. After he had stayed with John when I rushed to Florida for my business trip, Happy came into the Airstream with me when I returned to North Carolina. He settled in immediately, selecting under the bed as his favorite place to sleep as I had known he would.

On our first travel day together, I needed to go back to the dealer to have some work done. I had purchased a tent-style dog pen that went all the way across the back seat. Happy has his litter box and food and water back there. After unhitching the Airstream at the dealer, I parked beside the building in the shade. It was a beautiful, cool day. Happy ate and napped in the back seat while I worked at the computer in the front seat. The work took most of the day, but things seemed to be going well.

That night I heard Happy's stomach start to rumble. Gas in a rabbit is a very bad sign. A rabbit with uncomfortable gas won't eat.

I went out and bought some gas medicine. Rabbits use the same gas medicine as human babies. I didn't have any feeding formula because Happy had never been sick. I crushed up some of his food to feed to him in a water slurry. The next day Happy still wasn't eating or drinking, and he wasn't moving very much either. Had I killed him from the stress of one day sitting in the car? It had been such a beautiful day, and he had seemed well that day, eating and playing and sleeping like normal.

I called around to veterinarians and was told emphatically by each "No rabbits!" There was a rabbit specialty hospital about an hour away, so I made an appointment there. That day I was checking out of the RV park, so I hitched up and took the Halfloaf with me.

The rabbit hospital had told me I could bring the trailer into their parking lot, but when I got there I saw that I would take up their entire lot. Driving around all of the side streets, I didn't find anywhere else to park. There was one church, but when I called the number on the sign, no one answered.

Someone finally asked if I was lost, and I explained my problem. He told me the restaurant on the corner was about to close for the afternoon, and the owner had a soft spot for animals. After some cooing over Happy by the restaurant owner, I ended up parking there.

Happy got some treatment at the hospital, and I got a pile of medications to take with me. Over the weekend, Happy didn't really improve, and I thought he was probably going to die. I had a reservation Monday at an RV park an hour on the other side of the rabbit hospital, so I drove back over and parked at the restaurant again. This time the vet decided Happy should be hospitalized for a few days.

When I got Happy back, he was an entirely new rabbit. Everything about his appearance, eating, and biological output had changed. It was apparent to me then that he had been steadily declining toward his crisis for at least three months. The decline had been almost imperceptible, and what I did notice I had thought was just the inevitability of old age. Now that Happy was recovered, we were ready to go on the road.

Living in the RV, I'm acutely aware of every moment of his day. The RV does cause some more stress, but I'm not sure he'd still be alive if we weren't living this close. There is no chance of any unperceived decline.

I do have to be very careful with him though. He can really only handle two moderate days of driving back-to-back, and then we need to rest. He can't take temperatures over 75 for very long. My illness has pretty much the same requirements, so we're a good match. We had probably overdone it a bit driving across California and then all the way around Lake Tahoe in two days.

When we travel, I stop every hour and feed him some lettuce. I've also found that he goes into a bit of a road trance, but picking him up and petting him seems to help him come out of his trance. The one time I ran out of lettuce, he had a little gas the next day that quickly passed with medication and plenty of servings of yummy lettuce.

Happy recovered in Carson City without having to get additional support from a vet. We did stay a little longer than planned for him to rest though. I moved from the casino to an RV park for a few days.

CHAPTER 30

Life and Death
on the Pony Express

I HAD CHOSEN TO TAKE "AMERICA'S
Loneliest Highway" out of Carson City, not realizing that
it followed the Pony Express Trail. About 15 years earlier my mother had ridden the Pony Express Trail from
San Francisco to St. Louis and, two years later, from St.
Louis to San Francisco. She had been a lifelong horse-
woman, a founder of the California Dressage Society
and, with my dad, a frequent participant in 50 and 100
mile horse events called "endurance rides."

The first time she had been bucked off near

the beginning of the trip. She couldn't walk but she could still ride, so she rode to California and then saw a doctor. It turned out that metastatic breast cancer had weakened her pelvis. When she was bucked off, her pelvis had cracked. Her expected lifespan was less than two years.

She had metal rods inserted in her leg bones preventatively so that if she were thrown from her horse again, the bones would stay together. Eventually, that's exactly what happened—she was thrown from her horse, and she cracked her femur. After an x-ray confirmed the break, she took an aspirin and kept going.

The second time she rode the Pony Express Trail, the pictures show her thin and visibly weakened. Refusing crutches, she held onto a tall hiking pole when she walked. Soon after, her body shut down. She could no longer eat, and within a couple of weeks, she went from a woman who rode horses every day to dead.

The Pony Express Trail had meant so much to her, and it hadn't crossed my mind that it was a place that I would find myself more than a decade later. To me, the Pony Express Trail was a remote place that you accessed by horseback over weeks and weeks. It never occurred to me it was a place that I could drive to.

Now I was the one facing failing health, though much more slowly. I have lived a wonderful life and done things that with my current ill health I can no longer do. I have traveled to the Soviet Union and later to the nations that emerged out of that region and to Europe, China, and India. I once flew to Hawaii just get a continuing education certificate.

I have a bowl of finisher medals from half-marathons and sprint triathlons. I owned paintings that few people get to enjoy in their homes. The joys of those purchases and those years I lived with those things can never be taken away from me. My travels will live with me always. I cherish my athletic accomplishments.

I used to be very afraid of disability in old age. My mother and grandmother had the best possible end-of-life and death experiences. They had children to manage their care, a certain amount of luck in the course of their decline, and lots of money to purchase the best available comforts. Being disabled as a younger person means I will have none of these things.

I could have had children, but I didn't because even in my twenties things weren't quite right with my body, and I was still recovering from the trauma of my earlier years. I was concerned about whether I could manage. Plus, children were just never my calling.

Security to keep one's same lifestyle from the peak of life until death is often sold as the only way to have happiness. But for me all of that is gone. I don't expect to have a long retirement. Even if Social Security still exists in its present form, it likely won't be much of a benefit to me. My 401(k), sold to me for years as the ultimate security, won't last long if I'm too sick to have an income.

Entrepreneur and writer Penelope Truck wrote,

"Money is not a goal, but a tool to reach a goal. Force yourself to want something meaningful for your life. People who focus on goals get them; people who focus on money get high anxiety." We live in a time of high anxiety.

There is a certain kind of terror in the pressure to be able to take care of yourself through any illness, when the fact is that you simply won't be able to do it. The health insurance that costs thousands of dollars per year to maintain will be gone as soon as you are truly in need. I've been able to keep mine for now, but at over $6,000 per year I'm not sure how much longer I can go on.

There was a woman at Columbia University who dragged her bed everywhere she went as a statement about the rape she had experienced. I too am dragging my bed everywhere I go. I didn't mean to be making a statement about the costs of illness and of healthcare, but just by surviving I am.

My relationship with money has changed. No reasonable amount of saving can support a long-term illness. There is no security in your 401(k). A friend squealed that I had become someone who works to live rather than lives to work. But that isn't it at all. I'm working to die.

It's not that I expect to die extremely soon, though at one point I did. In my worst year, I could feel myself dying. I was being subdivided into a dozen medical specialties, no one of which found me very sick, and it was as if I were dying right in front of them, and they couldn't see. My heart rhythm issues were mild as far as heart rhythm issues go, same for neurology, ophthalmology, and the rest. As a whole, my body was breaking, but the parts were merely fraying.

Through the determination to find treatments for the basket full of symptoms, the fraying has turned into a very slow unraveling. I no longer have the sense that my body is in the midst of being broken, but that it has been broken. My job is to make the best of what I have left, for as long as I can. There's nothing in particular about my illness that indicates a dramatically shortened life. But one doesn't really hear of people who have had ill health making it to 90.

Meanwhile I have this. This travel, this Pony Express trail, this free camping in the national forest. In actuality, moving into the RV hasn't changed my housing expenses very much. When you add together the costs of RV parks when they are needed, the loan on the Expedition, and the gas required to move the Halfloaf from place to place, the total almost exactly matches my former mortgage.

What costs less is no Starbucks down the street, no Jones family next door, no familiar landscape of stores, and nowhere to put whatever I might purchase anyway. I also have the security of being able to drive away from my few expenses. There is no house to sell, no art to commission out.

I haven't lost my sense of security, but where I find my security has changed. If I insisted it still be in the house, or it still be in my bank accounts, I would be terribly unhappy. My security now is in the wheels under my house. I would never have lived the life I have lived or become an entrepreneur if I couldn't find happiness in risk and change. Part of the allure of the nomad life is that it is enough stimulation to become engrossed in the "now." Without that stimulation, everything becomes about the past and the future, from hoarding family heirlooms to saving the money that will be consumed by your final illness.

Later I walked in the ruts of the Santa Fe Trail. What both trails share is that they are a graveyard. Those who died in travel were buried directly under the trail so that the weight of passing wagons would harden the soil and protect the graves. When you walk in those ruts, you are walking directly on the loss those immigrants experienced and into the loss the indigenous people of the land experienced. The loss is massive and sorrowful.

I had thought of the Santa Fe Trail as one set of wagon ruts, reflected in so many paintings of a single line of wagons trailing off to the horizon. One single path of loss and of triumph to walk. In fact, the Santa Fe Trail is generally at least four tracks wide. The multiple tracks allowed the wagon trains to stay bunched together for security. Later, the trail was so full that it blocked the migratory route of the buffalo. It must have looked like an invasion of extraterrestrials as all of the excess pressure from Europe was released out onto the plain, eventually pushing the indigenous people to the corners of the earth.

Where I walked, at least six tracks were still identifiable in a farmer's field. There was a historical marker beside the road with a place to pull in. The farmer had installed a small gate and put up a sign welcoming the public to come walk on the land.

There was a time in my life, after an extraordinary personal trauma, when I dared myself to die everywhere I went. I dared myself to jump off a sky lift. I dared myself to drive into a bridge. My life is now turned on its head. Fatigue looks like death. It feels like death. But as I traveled across America and walked over these unmarked graves, I dared myself to live.

CHAPTER 31

A Week on a Colorado Mountain

WHEN MY LIFE WAS EASY, I USED TO LIE ON my patio furniture and look at the sky and remind myself that the blue sky would always be free. Now that life is more difficult, that has proven to be true. The rules are set up so that an ill person is meant to be pitied. The sickest among us are allowed to survive, usually destitute, an opportunity for charity. Using illness to launch a lifestyle that inspires envy is not what you're supposed to do.

Yet less than a week after crossing America's Loneliest Highway, I was parked at the top of a mountain outside Dolores, Colorado. I hadn't seen another person on the 8 miles of forestry road I had driven. As far as I knew, there wasn't another person for 6,000 acres. For the first time since moving into the Halfloaf, I spent a day naked and tried my outdoor shower.

Where I once ran half-marathons and competed in sprint triathlons, now I can barely walk far enough to get out of sight of the Halfloaf. Still, it felt good to walk as far as I could and spin around and see almost nothing but forest.

A good friend asked why I was there, since I had never struck him as a nature lover. And I'm not. I like people. I like Starbucks. I like cities. But the forest is free. There's the practical side to that, keeping expenses down. But there's also a spiritual side.

My illness has brought grief into my life, but the principal trauma of my illness is fear. Here, that fear is set aside. It isn't true that I can live on nothing forever. Six figures put into the Halfloaf and the Expedition brought me to this place. But for a moment, life is free.

Entrepreneurs succeed by setting a price on their time and bringing in that value. Being ill and watching your price become uncertain means losing. It means losing your value, your ability to support yourself, your purpose in a transactional world. As an entrepreneur, my attention is always on what kind of value I am bringing in. In other words, my attention is on the very thing that as an ill person causes my terror.

The year I moved into my RV, the terror was at a

fever pitch across the country. One of the votes on health-care had left me sobbing in the middle of a work meeting. Though I didn't specifically flee to the woods because everything had become so awful, once I was there, it clear that it was one of the most rational responses pos-sible. Sitting here in the forest—if this is the end of my life, or of the life of the nation, or if I'm about to go bankrupt—what a glorious way to spend these days.

Being in an RV removes you from the framework where everything has economic value. Some people get confused by the joy this creates and fancy that all real RVers must be libertarians, believing in some kind of ultra-free market. That's not it at all. It's the dissolving away of the market. The market is left in town. I am up here on a mountain, removed from anyone's balance sheet.

My time here has no value; it is simply mine. It is mine in totality whether I am sick or well. Nothing changes. I've mentioned "ranch time," a time that was so different from the time we experienced in town that it felt as if the entire world had become an odd size. Now I know it's not about the ranch; it's about being closer to the earth. It was somewhat surreal to cook my meals and take my showers so far in the woods. Without an RV, this isn't something I could experience. It would be a place that would belong only to hikers and other healthy people.

I hadn't meant to be on that mountain. I had meant to be in Moab, Utah, still enjoying the wonderful grocery store with the Starbucks inside, the restaurants, and the national parks close by. However, just as I reached Moab, spring crossed over into summer, and it was too hot for me to boondock. To venture into the national parks with their questionable Verizon signals, I needed to stay to the weekend, and Moab RV parks were just too expensive to stay several days.

A weather map showed Dolores as the closest cool place. I had selected a national forest road documented online by other boondockers, but as I was driving toward it, I passed another turnoff with a sign that said "National Forest Access" and randomly decided to take it. The first camping spot I had found was a large meadow that overlooked a bog with various attractive plants and aspen trees, which I love. But as I dropped into the meadow from the road my Verizon signal had gone to zero.

Then there were no choices along the road for so long I was starting to think I had made a big mistake. The road had drainage dug into each side, so even if there was an opening in the trees the little moats prevented me from reaching it. Eventually I reached a little side-road where I found my spot. When I left, I decided to experiment and drove even further up the road, where I found that the very top of the mountain had a beautiful pond, good Verizon coverage, and plentiful camping spots. Ah well.

Some people would want a larger rig than I have so that they can spend longer in the woods. At one point I thought I wanted that. But I don't need more water or more electricity because what runs out is my ability to live on my own. Because I always eat all the best food on the first day, I'm completely bored with my food after a few days. More than that, I'm bored with myself.

Also, I underestimate how much boondocking takes out of me. I feel completely comfortable, but monitoring my electricity, monitoring my food, monitoring my tanks, monitoring my perimeter, all of it takes a toll on me. My goal is to spend an average of $20 a night on RV parking. My six nights on the side of the mountain earned me six nights at a $40 a night RV park. It was time to go find one and have a long sleep.

CHAPTER 32

Medication Management
at Mesa Verde

I HEADED TO A CAMPGROUND OUTSIDE MESA
Verde National Park where I was meeting up with Tara
again. When I was in elementary school, one of my
textbooks had a photo of a Mesa Verde cliff dwelling
on the cover, and I had always wanted to see that view
for myself. When I moved into my RV, I had only two
specific goals for the first year: get to California where I
could see my dad and go to Mesa Verde.

I had decided not to stop at Hovenweep National
Park on my drive to Colorado. The RV park at the visitor

center didn't have electric hookups, and it was too hot for
Happy and me to stay without air conditioning. I would
have to backtrack to leave, which is the worst. And it
was too far to drive for something I wasn't certain about.
Arriving at the sign for Hovenweep, I turned in anyway.

The people who had told me about Hovenweep
were 70-year-old hikers I had met at a diner outside Cap-
itol Reef National Park. The small diner was packed for
breakfast, and I had invited them to share my table.

The wife had been living out of a backpack for
three weeks with her husband joining her for the last
week after buttoning up the family home in Idaho. I
explained that I probably wouldn't be able to go where
they went and asked what I might be able to see from the
road. They assured me I would be able to see something,
but I got the impression that what you could see from
a road, any road, wasn't something they thought a lot
about.

The drive was much further than any map possibly could have indicated, and the hot flat desert much
hotter than the weather report could convey. After a
few miles on the terrible road, however, I was grimly
committed. Hitting a twisted old cattle guard, my trailer
shook so violently I stopped to check that my hitch was
still attached. When I finally reached the visitor center, I
cleaned up the contents of my refrigerator that had scat-
tered on the floor, put Happy in the trailer with the fan
on high and went in. A paved trail from the visitor center
went out to a few ancient dwellings, so the effort had not

been a total waste.

On the drive I also had a chance to stop at the Anasazi Heritage Center outside Dolores. Next, I was eager to achieve my near-lifetime dream of seeing Mesa Verde National Park. The problem was that one of my knees had gone on strike while I was on the mountain and didn't seem intent on coming back any time soon.

Tara is a car enthusiast with a sporty Porsche and happily drove us all around Mesa Verde. There was no way I could do a tour of a cliff dwelling under the best of circumstances. The tour was one to two hours long and required climbing up on actual cliffs with handmade wooden ladders.

We had planned ahead of time, before the knee problem, that I would sit on a lawn chair and read a book while she did the tour. I don't know what the experience of doing the tour was like, but I know I got the much rarer experience of sitting in silence and stillness on that ancient mesa and experiencing the woods and the winds much as the people who built those dwellings would have.

The overlooks that allowed one to see the dwellings were uneven and difficult to get to. While some had pretty bad ramps, others had nothing but stairs. Sometimes I had to crawl. Tara scrambled down them and then called back if it was worth using up my energy. One of them was down some stairs, required a walk on an uneven path, and then a second set of stairs. "Definitely worth it," was the report. I limped down and found myself looking at exactly the scene I remembered from childhood! This was what I had come to see.

Over a few days, we also drove back to the Anasazi Heritage Center so she could see it too and then we drove out to Four Corners.

Taking a break back at the RV park, where our identical Airstream Sport 16s were parked next to each other, it was time to count out my pills. I carry two bins of pills and some others that don't fit in the bins tucked away here and there. In my less than 100 square feet of living space, finding room for them is quite a commitment.

When I count out my pills, I close all my blinds first. I'm concerned about someone seeing me with so many pills and making a scene. I'm also a little cautious about who sees me take my pills. In some states a prescription medication cannot be outside of the pharmacist's bottle except when it is "in use." A prosecutor in Maine even took it upon himself to go after people who remove their pills from the bottle. And don't expect the police to know the law. I've seen law enforcement claim that prescription medications have to be in the pharmacist's bottle even in states where that isn't the law.

It takes me an hour to sort out all my pills for the week. I turn on a TV show and go through each of my boxes, sorting the pills into three extra-large pill boxes with a little well for each day of the week. The time it would take to do that several times a day, in addition to the risk of medication errors, makes pulling out pills as I use them impossible. Using pill boxes, on the other hand, allows me to keep nearly 100 percent compliance with a very complex medication regimen.

Meanwhile, the hysteria about drugs is building real risk for people with medical conditions. This year a news report showed a pile of small, new syringes at a remote campsite as a sign that "deviant" (yes, we're in the 1950s all over again) druggies were taking over the national forest. They may have been used for street drugs, but the trash more likely belonged to a diabetic person. At least two mobs have gathered to roust the urban homeless, and militias have declared it their duty to patrol public lands. With people like this roaming around, a chronic illness may be deadlier than it first seems.

In addition to the problems of whether it is socially safe to keep medications in an RV, no one can tell me if it's medically safe. There seems to be an assumption that every last person on medication lives in a middle-class American home with air conditioning and adequate heat. One of my medications is considered important to national defense, and so a very detailed study was made of its storage requirements. It was found to be stable in high heat for up to two years. Everything else I take? Almost no information available. I have been advised that putting my pills in the refrigerator won't help because then there will be a humidity problem. In any case, even if I dedicated my refrigerator to pills, they wouldn't fit.

Non-prescription medications have even less information available. Because of the Dietary Supplement Health and Education Act of 1994, many medications are exempt from the regulations that affect prescription drugs in the United States. Part of the push for the act was to ensure access to medications that may not find biotechnology industry sponsorship for the required research and validation. Of course, leaving these drugs off that route means they aren't covered by insurance. My insurance company has a payment process, but as near as I can tell, all documents sent to that process are dropped into a cave and never seen again. My documents have never been acknowledged, much less paid or denied. Consequently, the approximately $6,000 a year I pay for my non-prescription medications has an effect on access too!

And that does not even get into the complete shit-show that is cannabis regulation. Given my health conditions, it is possible cannabis may have a positive effect on my health. But that's not even something I want to know. If it were effective, it would be devastating to the life I've created for myself. At the time this paragraph was written, it would mean changing my domicile to another state and establishing a new network of insurance coverage and health care providers. It would mean drastically limiting and structuring my travel. My boyfriend, my business, everything would be thrown up in the air in order to access effective medication.

Each week when I count my pills, I am reminded

that these difficulties will exist in my life forever. Something could happen so that I don't have access to these pills I take daily, which would make my life more difficult. I survive on the edge of a cliff, and it wouldn't take much of a push to put the medications I rely on out of my reach. I'm fine with it most of the time, but sometimes the fear wraps around my heart and I cry a bit.

CHAPTER 33

Pagosa Springs
and Perfect Places

LOOKING AT MY MAP TO FIGURE OUT WHERE
I was going to go after Mesa Verde, I learned about a
place called Pagosa Springs. I had never heard of it, and
I wasn't sure if it was going to be a bust. It sounded like
a half-way defunct little hot springs town hidden in a
valley where there might not even be Verizon coverage.

The valley where I grew up had a hot spring.
In the previous century, it had even been a place some
tourists went. When I was a very small child, someone
rigged up a pipe feed from a hot spring to an old water

trough and I got to play in the water, but that was the only time I had ever been in a hot spring. I was eager to try this again and made a reservation at one of the spas.

Because I had paid for the spa reservation and didn't want to be stuck in a situation where I was trying to bring my trailer into a spa parking lot, I also made a reservation at an RV park outside town. Knowing where I was going to be, I had a few packages sent there too.

When I got to the park, it was stunningly beautiful. Situated at the start of the grade, Wolf Mountain soared overhead, and a mountain lake stretched out beside the campground. And there was absolutely no Verizon service.

I went in to settle up, expecting to pay a one-day cancelation fee, which was more than fair and would hopefully lead to my packages being accepted. Surprising me, she refunded all of my money and agreed to accept the packages at no fee. If I were living a different life, I would have stayed at that RV park forever.

Instead I found one closer to town. This one had Verizon coverage and overlooked a river. Closer to town, the mountains weren't quite so majestic. I drove across town to the main grocery store, which was better than anything I had seen in at least a thousand miles.

The quaint town was squeezed into a hillside with old streets and not very much parking. I learned later how beloved this town is by full-time RVers, but it wasn't really accessible to me. No matter, the next morning I showed up at the spa for a massage and a soak in the hot springs at the Springs Resort & Spa. This is where I would find my greatest bliss in the course of the year.

People have been trying to monetize the amazing mother spring since European settlement, but nothing had ever really gotten off the ground. Then, in the 1990s, sisters Nerissa and Keely Whittington purchased the property. In this era, the hillside was terraced into 23 pools. Each pool is fed directly from the spring at a different rate, resulting in a variety of temperatures. Employees scurry around the hillside updating the sign at each pool showing the current temperature. The current temperatures are also always available on the spa's website.

Because the pools are continually fed with water and are regularly emptied and cleaned, the water is not treated. This is the water that surges directly up from deep in the earth. You can dip in this pool for a bit, and then that one. And then lie around. Or go and soak your feet in the Pagosa River.

Even after taking a shower, the smell of the minerals remained in my skin and transferred to the sheets of my bed. For the next few days, each time I went to bed, I was transported back to my most blissful place. I don't know what to think about the supposed medical value of the water, but for me it was perfect.

This contrasted with my earlier stay on the ocean in Pacifica, just down the coast from the Golden Gate Bridge. I had thought the energy of the ocean was something I wanted, but my body isn't well enough to absorb that kind of energy, and it left me feeling exhausted.

I feel bad for not appreciating my two weeks on the ocean. The spot seemed so perfect that I keep thinking that I should go back for a month even as I realize that the crashing waves drained my energy. It just wasn't right for me. A person who doesn't move wouldn't know that. What if someone with chronic fatigue lived in an ocean-front condo and was feeling worse and worse? How would they ever know they might feel better if they packed up and moved inland? I don't think feeling better away from the ocean is what someone would usually expect.

For me, the same sort of difference exists between the desert of the southwest and the greenery of Florida. Many people love the otherworldly nature of the desert. For people with illnesses, the pure air and the absence of stimulation can be a perfect match. But for me, the desolation sinks into my soul and I feel like I can see my own skeleton desiccating in the sun. If I'm going south, it is the exuberant foliage of Florida that breathes life into my body.

I didn't truly understand, until I found my own perfect place, that there is no one place where the energy is the very best for sick people. That some of the places extolled for their healing powers might be completely wrong and harmful for some people. Moving every few weeks turned out to be an unexpected way to dial in on exactly where my body can be as well as possible.

CHAPTER 34

And Then I Skipped Some Stuff

WHEN I LEFT PAGOSA SPRINGS, MY GOAL WAS to make it into Kansas, which was on the outside of how far I'm capable of driving in a day. I had spotted a place on the other side of the mountain where I planned to take a nap on National Forest land. If I wasn't feeling up to finishing the drive that day, I could spend the night there or perhaps even stay through the weekend.

It would be the last place I would be able to stay off-grid for the rest of the year. The summer heat had come in, and Happy and I needed air conditioning during the day. For the rest of the year, we would stay in squares mapped out in RV parks, but today we would sleep wherever we found a space.

After driving over the mountain, I found the forest road turn-off and drove into the woods. There were more RVs already set up along the road than I would have expected, but eventually I found a spot where the side of the road dropped into a small, flat clearing overlooking a river. I snuggled into my bed for a nap under the pine canopy.

When I woke up, I smelled smoke. It was only a little bit of smoke, and it could have been someone's lunch cooking, but I only knew of one road in, and I was leaving anyway, so I packed up quickly just in case. I started driving back the way I had come in, and soon billowing smoke appeared in the sky. I sped up toward the fire and the only way out.

No one else was packing up. They were sitting in their lawn chairs. As I got near the fire and could see the red flames, I passed a travel trailer sitting unhitched, the owners drinking beer and watching the firefighters.

Firefighting equipment was parked on the road, with perhaps fifty crew members scurrying around like ants. The equipment was mainly parked along one side. I assumed it was in everyone's interest that people leave, so I asked the nearest firefighter if I could drive through. He checked on his radio, and I got the clearance. I threaded carefully through the equipment and sped away. I didn't slow down for an hour until I found myself squealing through a town with a 35 mph speed limit.

I continued on toward Kansas. Because of the summer heat, there would be no more naps or driving breaks for the rest of the year. I dislike hamburgers, but I quickly learned a chain that I especially loathe was the chain that always seemed to have an empty field next to it perfect for RV parking. When I stopped for lunch at one of their locations, I left the car running for Happy and locked the door from the outside with a key.

As a young woman, I drove with friends across the country in a car in three days. I regularly see RVers who can do it in five. They usually don't, but they will do things like wake up in Nashville and go to sleep in Dallas as if it were nothing. For me that trip would take nearly a week. I just can't drive that far, and I can't drive every day.

When I first got the RV, I thought I would make huge mileage over Friday, Saturday, and Sunday and then spend most of the week in one spot. It turned out that I can't do huge mileage, and Happy can't travel three days in a row. When I need to get somewhere far away, such as from Texas to California, it has worked better for me to travel a moderate distance one or two days in a row and then rest for a couple of days and catch up on work.

My goal now was North Carolina. It took me two days of driving to get from Pagosa Springs to Dodge City. On the way, I saw a guard tower beside the road and a sign to a historical site. I turned in and found myself at the Amache internment camp, where Japanese-Americans had been imprisoned during World

War II. That somber place was my only stop on the two days of driving.

I'm sure I passed a lot of things people would have liked me to have stopped and visited. One of them was Great Sand Dunes National Park. Let's talk about that for a minute, because people like to give me advice about where to stop. It's a special kind of unsolicited advice.

It's maddening how far wrong unsolicited advice can be. Not wrong in that it is bad advice, but wrong in that it has no relationship to the real world at all. I once posted a joke about fruit flies in my RV and a random person told me to put my fruit in my refrigerator. I don't eat fruit; there is no fruit. What are you even talking about? That's how unsolicited advice generally goes.

I could have said that I don't eat fruit, but it would not be a very funny joke if I had to explain everything in my kitchen to tell it. The poetics of a story would be destroyed if the story had to defend against every "well, actually" possible.

But that has become the life we lead in the era of social media. Each individual person may think their contribution is unique and special, but the result in our connected world is a tsunami of advice that crowds out the possibility of connection. Everything you say can be picked apart, and the picking takes away the enjoyment of sharing your life. This is part of the reason I wrote a book instead of a blog.

This is partly driven by the reality TV culture

that includes popular RVer YouTube channels. The fact that some people make their personal life decisions into a content business can confuse people into thinking that it is appropriate for them to have a vote in my life or that making my travel interesting to them is some kind of duty.

Earlier in the year I had driven past New Orleans without stopping. Recounting my route at some point, a man heard this and became enraged. He didn't even know me! No matter that had been the night before Mardi Gras and that I am quite ill. I've seen over and over again how admiration can turn to viciousness in an instant if I don't satisfy other people's travel fantasies.

In the minds of some people, living in an RV reduces your humanity. Instead, you become certain people's "spirit animal." While they stay at their home, their spirit wings away to the places you visit. If you won't go the places their spirit wants to go, their spirit is going to try to grab you by the hair and drag you there.

CHAPTER 35

Labor Day Weekend
in Dodge City

FOR THE MOST PART, I DON'T MAKE RV PARK reservations. This offends some people on social media who will argue that I can't possibly be getting into RV parks without reservations. And yet here I am.

Part of the disconnect is that the Halfloaf is only 16 feet long. When I left Pagosa Springs there were plenty of RV spaces left for a rig my size. And yet on YouTube I saw someone with a fifth wheel say that there were absolutely no spaces left in the entire region.

Being in a 16-foot travel trailer is a very different

experience from living in a fifth wheel. An RV park once put me in a corner and ran an extension cord from another site to fit me in. I have made reservations for holidays and crowded areas, but I have never once found that they were actually necessary. I may not have been able to stay in my first choice, but there has always been a place to stay that wasn't a Walmart parking lot.

Leaving Pagosa Springs, I had my eye on a few places to stop for the night but waited until I was closer to one before calling and making a reservation. The next day as I drove toward Dodge City, I called ahead to make another reservation there. It was Memorial Day weekend.

I had intended to stay only one night because the rates around Dodge City are a little high for rural Kansas. But when I called the park, they offered me an extremely low rate for an electric-only site. I changed my plans from staying just one night to staying the entire weekend. I had no idea what Dodge City had to offer, but holiday weekend reservations still felt a bit like a game of musical chairs, and I had just won.

When I got there, the park was half empty. The site I was given was actually a full hookup site. I was on the honor system not to use the water or sewer in the middle of the night. Let me say again, this was Labor Day Weekend! There are people who will say that the entire country doesn't have enough RV spaces and that there is nowhere to stay on a holiday weekend. These people have never been to Kansas.

I didn't know anything about Dodge City, and I hadn't been planning to stay there, so I picked up every single tourist pamphlet in the rack by the front door when I checked in. It turns out that a nonprofit in Kansas has a fabulous program called "The Eight Wonders of Kansas" which lists the eight best things to see in Kansas in a variety of categories.

Now that I had decided to stay, the first thing I needed to do was catch up on chores at my desk. Saturday morning, as soon as quiet hours were over, I unhitched. This is one of the most physically demanding tasks of living in a travel trailer. If I can, I wait until I am rested and the temperature is cool and do it in the morning. I move very slowly so I don't get too hot or wear myself out, and eventually it gets done. Later, after succumbing to heat intolerance for the umpteenth time, I purchased an ice vest to wear while I unhitch.

Usually I just use my tanks for at least the first day and don't hook up my water and sewer, another physically demanding task, until the next day. In this case there would be no water and sewer. When I was able to get water and sewer a week later, it went very badly and demonstrated the need for that ice vest.

Saturday, I stayed at my desk most of the day and also did my laundry at the park facilities. Since I had no water connection, I also took a shower at their facilities. I dislike public showers for the most part, but theirs were clean and roomy.

Sunday, I decided to start the day by going to

church. The oldest church in continuous use in Dodge City is St. Cornelius Episcopal Church, which was built in 1898. My two other main stops were going to be Fort Larned and The Big Well, if my energy held up to do both.

In these smaller communities, the activities of daily life and the activities of a "tourist" can be one and the same. You can experience the community without wearing yourself out on tourist activities. Just getting an oil change can be an introduction to the community. Here, I went to church.

The church had a small congregation. I wouldn't usually get tangled up in coffee hour, but I needed to go through to the hall restroom to change from church clothes into tourist clothes. I learned that the priest who had led the service was a local man whose mother was very proud of him. Everyone was terribly friendly, but I was eventually able to tear myself away and drive to Fort Larned.

Fort Larned National Historic Site preserves a small historic fort. It's actually the fort where the "Buffalo Soldiers," the black soldiers who were sent out West after the Civil War, were based. Given its diminutive size, one would think it might be disability-friendly. Even on Memorial Day Weekend, the parking lot was mostly empty, so there was no jostling with a crowd.

But the parking lot is situated more than an eighth of a mile away from the buildings. I had thought to go to the visitor center and then leave, but arriving at the buildings, it wasn't at all clear where the visitor center might be.

When I'm in a grocery store or a mall, I can sometimes see the desperation on the faces of people with illnesses like mine. Turning down the wrong aisle in the store or the wrong hall is like driving 20 miles the wrong direction with the gas gauge on "E." Now I was walking around the fort with no idea where to go.

By the time I found the visitor center, I was in pain and very grumpy. I wanted to express to these people that if only they had put out a sign, my experience would have been so much different. At the same time, it's too emotionally painful to try to explain that you're in pain and for someone not even to care about that. You can't ask people to care. There are just too many people and not enough caring. People who walk in front of you at the grocery store when you're trying not to fall down. People who won't stop their cars and let you cross the street when you're trying not to pass out.

The greeters forced an engagement, and I was too agitated over the situation to contain myself. I sputtered a bit about how far the walk had been and how sad it was that a site that had the potential to be so disability-friendly was so awful. It turned out to be worse than not being heard. They thought they were doing a great job. Hadn't I seen the wheelchair they left by the parking lot? I'm not sure how I was supposed to get myself an eighth of a mile on a gravel walkway with a transport wheelchair, but okay. Also, they had a golf cart running between the parking lot and the site. Well, they usually did, but the driver had gone on some kind of break, and they hadn't seen her in a while. Anyway, they were absolutely the best on accessibility.

Later a volunteer actor in the historical interpretation in the buildings I passed on the way back to my car kindly noticed I was in pain and asked if I was okay. Whatever goodwill that gained was lost when I started the walk back to the cars and noticed that the golf cart was just sitting in the parking lot. The driver took no notice of me as I hobbled the entire walkway right in front of her.

I didn't dare say a single word as I walked past her. I got in my car and decided what to do next. My puzzle when I decide to do something exhausting is whether to keep going or go home and sleep. After something like this, even if I take a nap, my ability to think usually won't return to normal until at least one overnight sleep. Since resting gets me nothing, if I'm feeling well enough sometimes it makes sense to do all the exhausting things in one day.

I decided to drive on to the Big Well. I also as a rule stop at all historical markers. Usually I can read those without getting out of the car.

At the Big Well, I was able to park right at the front door of the museum. Inside, the museum was small and had benches where I could sit and take in the displays on the wall. Visitors could walk the stairs to the bottom of the well, but that activity obviously was not for me.

The Big Well is the largest hand-dug well in the world. Back in the day, a railroad magnate had the idea that if he could provide water to people, they would come. It had worked for a time. Though the heyday of the Dodge City region was over, the small town of Greensburg remained clustered around the Big Well.

Then in 2007 the town was destroyed by an EF5 tornado. So soon after the horrors of Katrina, the federal government was determined to make this a FEMA success story. The town rebuilt as a sustainable town. All of the buildings are built to certain efficiency standards, and the entire town operates on wind energy. The Big Well museum was rebuilt not just as a tribute to the Big Well but also as a memorial to the destruction the tornado caused and a celebration of the rebuilding.

These two tourist attractions illustrate in one day the positives and negatives of going to second- or third-level tourist attractions. On the one hand, there's not an Uber available at a moment's notice or any other kind of convenience service. On the other hand, even on Labor Day Weekend I could park near the entrance to both locations, and I didn't have to fight my way through any sort of crowds.

This entire year, smaller towns proved to be more accessible to me simply because they were on a smaller scale. I went to downtown Fredericksburg instead of downtown Austin. I had researched going to Bernalillo instead of Albuquerque. I went to Morro Bay instead of Monterey. I went to Pacifica instead of San Francisco.

And finally, when I could have been in any city in America, I spent Labor Day weekend in Dodge City.

CHAPTER 36

The Last Corner of Housing Abundance

I WAS NEVER A MINIMALIST. I ONCE DATED A man who let his belongings deteriorate into rubbish—he called it "entropy"—and in my discomfort over watching his things clatter together and break, I discovered that I have a love for things. When I lived in a house, I collected original paintings and antique furniture and got great pleasure out of what I owned.

Nonetheless, the things I loved became covered in a layer of useless trash, as in most homes. I read Maria Kondo and got rid of the trash I hated. I leaned paintings against the walls in the corners of my house as a force field against trash piling up there again.

Even now, if I don't move for a few days, the trash piles up again. It's only the regular requirement to pack up my house that keeps it neat. The small size and the regular moves reduce the suffering my materialism causes me.

I have met extraordinary minimalists on the road. When I was leaving Florida, I stopped at a county park outside Cedar Key. My neighbor was a tent camper and very gregarious. I would talk to him and then I would go inside away from the bugs and lie down on my soft mattress and it seemed I lived an incredibly luxurious life.

I wasn't sure if he was a vacationer, so I asked him if he was full-time in his car.

"Oh no!" he said, taken aback. I was so embarrassed. Of course, he had a house, and I had just suggested he was homeless and somehow insulted him.

"I'm a full-time backpacker. I just use the car to move from one area of the country to another. I was in Texas before I came here."

I am not a minimalist, and yet like this man I am very close to not only having the minimum for myself but embodying the minimum in our world. We live in the nooks and crannies that would otherwise go unused. In a country where the available housing stock is bursting at the seams, we live in the abundance of other spaces that have been there all along.

When I was in San Francisco, I attended a fancy

dinner with a friend. I sat next to a woman who had been doing research as an advertiser for a big box store. When she learned that I live in an RV she said, "There are all these people in RVs who stay at Walmart. It's this huge thing and no one but RVers know about it. How do people find out about it?"

If I think very hard, I can remember that before I bought an RV I didn't know that anyone lived at Walmart. But in my life now it is impossible not to know. These extra spaces that were always waiting and invisible to me are now visible everywhere I look.

When I first got the Halfloaf, I was passing through the Research Triangle Park area on a drive from the mountains to the sea and needed to stop somewhere to spend the night. I stopped at a Cabelas that had a steak restaurant on one side of the parking lot and a Starbucks on the other.

A friend came out and we had a lovely dinner. I walked a few feet to bed and in the morning, I stumbled over to Starbucks for my breakfast. Beyond mere space, RVers have access to abundance. That abundance is not always appreciated.

When I was in Arizona, I stopped at the Twin Arrows Casino to sleep. The particular day of the week that I was there, the steak restaurant was closed but the buffet had an excellent roast. The Starbucks was open 24 hours. Parked directly under a streetlight in the parking lot, I even picked up some electricity overnight from my solar panel. I've never lived in a house within walking distance of a Starbucks, but in an RV, this was now my second time to be able to duck out for coffee and return to my desk.

The far side of the parking lot had an area for big rigs to spend the night, and as I pulled out in the morning, I saw a flatbed carrying a 16-foot Airstream just like the Halfloaf. I snapped a photo and posted it to the Internet, where I was promptly informed that real RVers don't spend the night in parking lots, even if there's a Starbucks. The real RVer who told me that would have had to drive a quarter of the way across Arizona without stopping rather than appreciate everything he had been given.

Now I was driving out of Dodge City toward a city park. I had already stayed at a few municipal parks on the trip. Some of them are even free for short stays, bringing grandparents and tourists to visit family or spend some money in town. This park was a lake with a campground split in two by a creek and a swath of trees. One side of the campground was inhabited by families with children splashing in a swimming hole and eating burgers at picnic tables. The other side of the campground was deserted except for one RV completely covered in white supremacist iconography and a truck decorated to match.

I hadn't noticed the family side of the campground when I drove in, so my choice was to park at this lake alone with the white supremacist or leave. I decided to stay. I picked the white supremacist. I read the instructions about what I was supposed to pay, and they made zero sense to me. I wasn't sure if I had to pay anything. I asked my neighbor, and he answered in a friendly way, so now he was my personal white supremacist. At night when men came roaring through the white supremacist side of the campground in jacked-up trucks, I would have felt intimidated were it not for the fact that I had my own redneck.

I'm still not sure what is going too far in taking advantage of the abundance offered to me, not just because I'm in an RV but as a white woman in America. I know how I look has an impact on just how much is available to me. Would a non-white RVer have felt comfortable staying where I did? Would they even have felt comfortable staying with the families on the other side of the trees?

My guess to each question is no, but remember to take advice only from people who have actually done something. My inclination is to put my discomforts onto people I see as even more vulnerable than I am. It is very much like men who put their discomforts onto me, certain that I must be thinking about safety all the time. I know that's not true about me, so why should I imagine I have any idea how members of other vulnerable groups feel?

There are non-white RVers out here. There are even several who have YouTube channels. If you are thinking about moving into an RV but have questions about just how much abundance is available to you, I would recommend asking someone who looks like you. What I can tell you is that many people from groups who might have fears about being out here because of how they look or some essential aspect of their lives report having the same experience of abundance that I have had.

CHAPTER 37

Overheated in Missouri

CONTINUING ON TO MISSOURI, I PULLED into an RV park outside Noel. This town is well known not just for its name, but for a strike at the chicken plant when 120 Somali workers walked off the job after not being allowed to pray. Management later said it was a misunderstanding, and the workers got their jobs back.

I took a wrong turn on the way to the RV park and ended up driving along an incredibly lush and treacherous road with rock formations leaning out over-head. The road led to that very chicken plant. It looked a bit more like a prison than an industrial site. Menacing signs indicated you would be in very big trouble for a lot of things. I turned around in the parking lot across the street, doing my very best to look like a lost RVer with a bunny and not like a chicken saboteur.

The RV park was adjacent to the Elk River. For a fee, the park would loan you a float and pick you up four miles downstream. I don't have the patience for that sort of thing, but I was ready to empty my waste tank and refill my water. It was impossibly hot, and someone had tightened the lid on the sewer opening like they were sealing in the contents of Fort Knox instead of their discarded poop. I called for help and waited.

I should have gone back into my trailer and stood under the air conditioner, but I felt like if I changed anything I would fall over. I just wanted to get this done and then I was going to go lie in the river. I sat at the picnic table.

After a while, someone came and opened the sewer cap with a wrench. I emptied my sewer tank and filled my water. Then I stumbled into my trailer and stripped off my soaking wet clothes. I was trembling and it was hard to get my swimsuit on. Fortunately, the river was only 50 yards away. Sinking into the slow-moving water, I put my sandals on my hands to protect from fishhooks and anchored myself on the gravel while I floated.

A lady who had recently moved to the area was sitting in a folding chair with her feet in the water, and we chatted about life. Eventually I was ready to get up. I tried to pull my feet under me, but my legs would not cooperate, and I felt a sharp pain in my knee. I cried out a swear word just as two children walked by. "Don't listen to bad words!" I said, as the children giggled.

I backed more toward the center of the river where I could get my legs under me and walked up out of the river. After the short walk back to my trailer, I had nothing left. The wet bathing suit went on the floor with my wet clothes, and I lay shaking in my bed. It was as if some kind of electric torture was pulsing through my body and buzzing in my ears.

The sound drowned out every thought in my brain. I couldn't watch a TV show or read a book. I just lay there helplessly for the rest of the afternoon until I finally fell asleep. When I got up in the morning, my body felt like I had climbed a high mountain. I had once climbed Mt. Katadin, the boulder-strewn mountain in Maine that marks the end of the Appalachian Trail. Now my body was equally destroyed by sitting at a picnic bench on a hot day.

A few days later, I was in Boone, North Carolina. I had thought that when I returned to North Carolina, I could stay in Boone for the summer. Boone has a humid continental climate, common in the Pacific Northwest but very limited in the South. It is usually at least 10 degrees cooler there than in the rest of the region. But I couldn't find an RV park with a good Verizon signal and had to move on. It was too bad because when I got to the park there, it was heavenly.

The woman who pulled in next to me was on a

long trip with her four-year-old son while her husband minded the house. They were returning from seeing the Synchronous Fireflies at Great Smokey Mountains National Park and on their way to tour Washington, DC. She was so fascinating that I wanted to talk to her more, but I didn't want to invade her space by sitting at her picnic bench.

After talking a while, I began to feel a strong pressure on the top of my head. I knew where this was going. Soon my vision was going black, I felt queasy, and the pressure was forcing me down. If I didn't get flat soon, I would pass out and fall down.

I stumbled back into my trailer and lay on my bed. My vision returned, but each time I sat up to do something, the pressure and the queasiness returned. Once again, I was lying in my bed, not quite well enough to watch TV or read a book. Once again, I lay in bed like that for several hours until I fell asleep for the night.

A while ago I had this experience whenever I got hot, but some treatments had reduced the frequency. Now I had had two episodes within a few days of each other. And the second time I wasn't even hot but had just stood for too long. I started to worry about how I was going to make it through the summer.

As long as I live within my limits, I forget that I am unwell. Sometimes it feels like I must be paranoid or some kind of exaggerator or faker. A few years earlier, when my health was rapidly deteriorating, my physician booked me an appointment with a mind/body therapist.

I met with her several times, and one of the key lessons I took away from those invaluable meetings was that I am a person with chronic illness. If I listen to my body, that's all it is. If I don't, I am a person who is exhausted and miserable.

Here was my reminder that the limits were still there. There are things I can't do. The best way to avoid all of these problems would be to "chase 75" as the RVers say, meaning drive to wherever it is 75 degrees. But those of us with chronic illnesses may be tied to our home base to qualify for medical insurance, to obtain medical care, and for other reasons.

I've mentioned that I have noise sensitivity, and the air conditioner in my trailer can be truly unbearable. Furthermore, RV air conditioners are only capable of cooling 20 degrees from the outside air. As the summer wore on and the heat radiated through the wall of my RV, it made for 80-degree afternoons inside. If I parked in the sun, I would have to lie on my bed unable to work for several hours each afternoon.

Hitching and unhitching in the middle of the day became impossible. Even the early mornings were too warm. I purchased an ice vest, which does help some. Instead of lying in bed trembling after unhitching, I may be able to lie in bed and watch TV or even do the dishes. But you won't find me reading or writing a book after the activity.

CHAPTER 38

The Displacement of Home Base

NOW IT WAS TIME TO DRIVE BACK TO Research Triangle Park. Nothing felt the same. In my road warrior days, I had experienced a similar displacement on arriving home. I remember driving behind a truck and being surprised that the phone number it advertised had the same area code as I did. When I got off the road and moved into a management job, I had an essay published on CNN.com about sitting on my couch for the first time. Despite owning a couch for years, I had never actually sat on it.

Now I was staying at the State Fairgrounds, just

a couple of miles from my old house. I went to my Starbucks and saw all my friends. They asked me about my trip, but where do you even start? "I drove across the country and back" says nothing. To say everything isn't even possible. This book isn't even a hundredth of what I experienced this year. I had experienced as much in this one year as in ten of my previous years.

The health problems that I had attributed to the heat kept coming. I started to be unable to predict whether my legs would work each time I stood up. Walking, I would suddenly feel like I was about to fall. Sometimes I had to will each step like some kind of robot. I got some treatment that improved the situation, but I started to seriously think about a mobility scooter. I had skipped all those cities. What if next time I could go more places?

Unfortunately, it didn't stop there. I started having pain in my arms that I had not previously experienced. The pain made it difficult to reach up. Fortunately, everything about hitching up requires reaching down.

I had learned to ask for help on the road, but now I had to ask for help at home. I went to a buffet lunch with business associates, and I had to ask someone to load my plate for me. I had been watching videos from a wonderful human being, Joy Ross, who is blind. She says she used to refuse to ask for help, but now she has many YouTube videos showing how she navigates the world by asking for help from many different people, and her example served as a model for me.

In very rural locations in the middle of the

country, I had found the food I could purchase tasteless.
The basil tasted like parsley, but I reasoned it had a hard
life. When I got home, nothing tasted as I remembered
it. My boyfriend took me to a popular brunch restaurant
that had seemed wonderful when I left but now seemed
plastic. Everything in the décor was made to look like
something else, and the food was beautiful but had absolutely no flavor. Informed by my vast experience in the
real America, I explained how these places were all fake.

Now that I was changing my medication for my
arm and leg issues, my sense of taste returned. The basil
had probably been fine. The brunch restaurant actually
did serve real food. I was the one who had been a little
bit out of sync.

My entire trip I had stayed on the Eastern Time
Zone so that traveling was seamless to my clients and
associates. Nonetheless, returning to the Eastern Time
Zone was difficult. In the West, I had been able to complete my work tasks for the day well before I had to deal
with physical tasks of the day such as moving the trailer.
Now everything that was required of me piled up.

The fairgrounds limited stays to two weeks. Next,
I could move out to the Thousand Trails in Advance for
two weeks. Then return to Jordan Lake, that beautiful
state park right in the heart of the cities that make up the
Triangle.

I tried to meet up with friends for lunch. I wanted
to see everyone. But I had to acknowledge that seeing
them hurt me. There was a gap between their lives and

mine that couldn't be closed. And as my days in the area continued on, I became exhausted. If I talked about what it cost me to meet with them, it made them antsy. No one wants to hear you're going to have lunch with them and then sleep for two days and risk losing all your clients and going broke. They want to imagine that their friendship has no cost.

I've never learned to talk about my illness in a way that works. Either I am impossibly cheerful, which is actually more or less how my personality is, and they cannot imagine that I suffer even as I am stating that I suffer, or I'm very serious about suffering and it's no secret that no one wants to be around that.

Leaving those problems aside, while I was home the Halfloaf needed to go in for service. Nothing much had gone wrong, but I had that long list of minor items to be fixed. It's also a good idea to have the roof inspected and the propane lines inspected. The dealer said it would take a week to complete my list. I moved my office into John's house and drove the Halfloaf up to the dealer's lot.

Driving away was bizarre. I had driven across the country and back and still slept in my own bed every night. Seeing the country is awesome, but there's also a lot to be said for always sleeping in your own bed no matter where you go.

Sitting in John's house, I thought of some of the choices I had made over the trip. Cities I hadn't gone to, beach boardwalks missed. I also thought of some of the challenges that would be coming up: work conferences, another winter in Miami with the boardwalk and Lincoln Avenue beckoning. I didn't want to miss out again. It was time to get some kind of mobility scooter or wheelchair.

So, I downsized again. My trailer and the back axle on my car were at their weight capacity. I thought about using a front hitch to carry the scooter, but for several reasons rejected the idea. The scooter I selected would have to go in the back of the car, which meant removing about 150 pounds of belongings.

The tall ladder came out. Over the year I had found that you don't often need a ladder, but when you need one, you really, really need one. Now I'll have to ask a neighbor. I still have a small ladder for getting into the back of my Expedition.

Out came three boxes of books. I'll have to mail books back and forth with my boyfriend more often. Out came a box of cooking pots I had never used, the outdoor table and outdoor rug I also never used and a folding chair. I kept two camping chairs.

When I saw the scooter, its name was obvious: Biscuit. And my car, which had resisted naming for the entire year, suddenly became amenable to Cherry Cupcake, Cupcake for short. Over the days of fall, I would be returning to the same places in Florida that I had been last year, but now I could have a different kind of adventure.

CHAPTER 39

A Sense of Accomplishment

UNTIL I WROTE THIS BOOK, I DIDN'T THINK of this as a year in which anything bad had happened in my life. The facts of the story reveal otherwise, but the joy in what I saw and the joy in my accomplishment is an avalanche that buries every rock and thorn.

The other day I heard someone say that she's teaching her children not to be entitled by teaching them that they have to earn everything, even their own bed. But all that does is foster the entitlement of "I earned it." None of us has earned the good fortune that we have. To suggest that we have would mean that disability isn't only a misfortune, it's an immorality.

I didn't earn my disability. And I didn't earn my beautiful year. Just after the year ended, as I was returning to Florida for the winter, I had an accident that could have killed me. My rig, Happy, and I are okay, but it could have happened on the Pony Express Trail under the blazing sun without another car to be seen for hours. At any moment, all of this can change.

Right now, I'm well enough to work. When I was healthier, accomplishment was a regular part of my life. I charged up the career ladder, targeting and obtaining the jobs I wanted. No matter what else was on the line, one thing I could do was work harder than everyone else.

I had been a distance walker and for a short time a runner, generally walking 12 miles per day and up to 26 miles around town on Saturdays. When the city's homeless men gathered at the downtown shelter, they would compare notes on the furthest places they had seen me and then tell me how impressed they were the next week when I passed them twirling signs for a few dollars. I enjoyed the few half-marathons and triathlons I did.

My illness took away my ability to have that sense of accomplishment. I no longer have a hard day's work well done to look back on. I mostly can't walk further than I can see when I start out. No one brags about my impressive physical feats. But moving into the RV changed that. I became someone doing interesting things again. After my first season of travels, I posted the map of my route on Facebook. My friends were astounded. I joked that they had been there, virtually, the entire way, so what was so astonishing. But looking at that map, I too was astonished.

My illness had the potential to take everything from me—my job, my home, even my sense of self-worth. Instead, I found a new job, a new home, and a new way to have a life I could look back on with pride. I did better than pride. I accomplished something I had never dreamed of.

Some people say that you have to have dreamed of living in an RV to enjoy it. I never thought of living in an RV until I had no other choice. The Halfloaf wasn't an answer to a dream, it was an answer to a need. I knew nothing about boondocking or moochdocking or any of the ways a person can get across the country when I bought my Airstream. All I knew was I needed to get to Florida for the winter.

Then I left Miami on the first day of February, returned to North Carolina on the last day of June, and in between drove across the country and back on my own. In those 22 weeks I drove 200 hours. If I had a five-day-a-week job, that would be equivalent of a commute that was 90 minutes each way. Or, as I had driven through the New Mexico scenery, over the Sierra Nevada mountains, and across the Pony Express Trail, was the time more equivalent to watching shows? American TV watching peaked almost a decade ago, but the average American streamed two and a half hours of content each day in the period of time I was soaking up the actual world.

When I reach out to grasp comparisons to the life I lived in the suburbs, the comparisons fail. This year I experienced something I had never experienced before. I experienced something which, even if I were to complete the same drive all over again, I would never experience the same way again.

Right now, I don't want to experience it again. It was an amazing time, but looking back on it as I write from my winter spot in Miami, that was a lot of driving. Some full-time RVers call this first year "vacation mode" and consider it a mistake. They try to encourage other people not to do it.

I don't regret it a bit. If life hands you an RV, why wouldn't you go on vacation? There was a point in my life when I sat in a doctor's office as she puzzled over the decline of my body and I thought *I am watching myself die*. It was only through a chance encounter at work that I learned the name of the disease that constituted a large segment of my illness and was able to get treatment that changed things a bit. It was only by chance that right now I don't feel like I am dying.

My goal is to do anything that isn't dying. There is nothing that has felt less like death than driving across the United States and back, driving at the pace of the life my body has given me.

ABOUT THE AUTHOR

MARY K.D. D'ROZARIO is a biotechnology professional with more than 20 years of experience in clinical research and product development. Her desk is in a 16-foot Airstream travel trailer located somewhere in America.

Made in the USA
Middletown, DE
15 September 2020